Behind the Hedgerows

by

John Francis Mahoney

Behind the Hedgerows

Published by Elgin Press

Overview of "Hedgerows"

When we arrived in Ireland, I knew instinctively that there would be many memorable experiences, and so I determined early on to record my observations.

In the beginning, those observations were pretty well limited to scenes and events. They were almost perfunctory because I had no real underpinning with which to interpret what I saw and heard.

As the journey progressed, I religiously recorded our activities, frequently writing as long as two hours a day. I realized within a couple weeks that my observations were taking on new dimensions. Not only was I describing people and events, I was also beginning to dissect the culture, to ask myself questions about the people and their habits. This led quite naturally to the next step in exploring the country. I wondered why the Irish were so... Irish?

I began to look at the Irish psyche played out before my eyes and ears each day. I began to plumb the sociology of the place. I questioned, in my mind, the relationship of the people to their government, their church and their neighbors.

From my vantage point at the University, I absorbed a great many articulate, descriptive insights into the Irish society.

Almost unconsciously, I was also beginning to come to grips with what I believe is a hedgerow mentality. I was on one side of the figurative fence, and the natives were on the other. I could observe their rituals, but I couldn't really understand them, much less participate in them.

Over the next ten months that would change dramatically. By recording my observations on a daily basis, eventually I was able to connect the dots, and patterns emerged that were, if not exactly transparent, at least only modestly opaque.

I began as "The Yank," grew into "the Professor", and eventually became "John". I started off as the outsider who couldn't even get through customs without a hassle and eventually was invited by several local farmers to join them as they took their mares up to a Tipperary stud farm. In short, I went from "in front of" to Behind the Hedgerows.

To Mary and Kate

About the Title

The hedgerow in Ireland is a cultural, political, and historic point of reference. When British colonial rule was imposed centuries ago, the hedgerow became a symbol of escape from the oppressors. It was behind the hedgerows that generations of Irish children were illegally introduced to the fundamentals of education and the oral culture of their people; it was behind the hedgerows that the forbidden Mass was surreptitiously celebrated, usually on a flat rock, and it was behind the hedgerows that thousands of Irish literally hid from the hangman.

When the Penal Laws were lifted and the Irish gradually began to repossess their stolen properties, the hedgerows (as well as stone walls) were redefined as the outer limits of a man's personal domain, the place he called his own, behind which no one ventured unless he was invited.

It was against this backdrop that I framed our experience in Ireland.

When we arrived at Limerick, we understood very little of the hedgerow mentality, and we knew relatively few people. The cosmopolitan atmosphere at the University, however, helped us in the transition from the States, and, once on campus, we had a vantage point from which to negotiate our way around the broader community.

That was a most fortunate circumstance, for we not only were invited behind the hedgerows, we were warmly welcomed.

Prologue

In the spring of 1990, I received a telephone call out of the blue from a gentleman named Malachy Glynn. He said he was representing the University of Limerick in Ireland. I had been to Limerick many times over the years and knew that there was no University of Limerick! After spending thirty years in Washington, D.C., however, I was still interested in hearing new approaches to old scams, and so I returned the call.

As it turned out, the former National Institute for Higher Education in Limerick had in fact been reconstituted as a bona fide University the previous year. On behalf of the new school, Mr. Glynn was anxious to secure an audience with the Speaker of the U.S. House of Representatives, Tom Foley.

The University, and particularly its College of Engineering, hoped to establish a working relationship with the Boeing Corporation, which is headquartered in Washington State. The Speaker, of course, was from Spokane. He was a natural contact, but they had no entré. Glynn had been told that I had access. Would I be willing to help?

I agreed to assist them and called the Speaker. At the appointed time, Glynn and Dr. Edward Walsh, the President of the University, flew over from Ireland for a meeting in the Speaker's office. It was a very productive gathering.

That afternoon, as we were touring the Capitol, Dr. Walsh said to me, "I'd give anything to have someone like you teaching at the University."

The bells and whistles went off in my mind. My wife Mary had been after me for ten years to get back into teaching. We had family ties to Ireland, had visited there frequently, and loved the country and the people. I thought this was a "natural." I went home and told her, "A funny thing happened to me on the way to the office today . . ." She never batted an eyelash.

"When do we leave?" she wanted to know.

Within a month, I had made contact with the University's College of Humanities, sorted out my business affairs, put our house on the market, and made a commitment to move to Ireland. At fifty-two years of age, I was going to test whether I was suffering from either mental sclerosis or social paralysis.

Summer 2002
Lake Ontario, New York

About the Author

For more than thirty years, John Francis Mahoney was deeply involved in national legislative issues. He spent a decade (1964-1974) as Administrative Assistant to Congressman James M. Hanley (D-NY), and he was a registered lobbyist in Washington, D.C, for more than fifteen years.

While maintaining a heavy engagement in practical day-to-day legislative politics, Mahoney also was active in academic circles, lecturing on contemporary government and the legislative process.

For nineteen years, he was a lecturer at Syracuse University's Maxwell School Washington Program. He was a founder and charter regent of the old Center for Congressional and Governmental Studies at Catholic University. He also traveled extensively as an active member of the bi-partisan Atlantic Association (now Council) of Young Political Leaders, which promotes international education, and cultural and political exchanges.

Over the years, he engaged successfully in a number of business ventures and hosted a weekly radio broadcast from Washington, D.C.

Mahoney earned a Bachelor's degree in Political Science from Le Moyne College in Syracuse, N.Y., and completed advanced studies toward a Ph.D. in the School of Politics at Catholic University.

He is an active member of the James Joyce Club, the Irish-American Cultural Institute, the Congressional Country Club, and Habitat for Humanity.

Monday September 3. After a delightful day of sightseeing and a memorable visit to the Quincy Market in Boston, my wife Mary, my daughter Kate and I took off from Logan Airport at about 7:50 p.m. As the wheels lifted off the ground, Kate suddenly broke down and sobbed her heart out. The poor kid had been holding it all in since early August, never actually believing that we would take her away from her house, her neighborhood, her friends, her school and church, and most of all, from Lady, our dachshund. She cried herself to sleep.

Tuesday, September 4. We arrived at Shannon Airport at 5:45 a.m. Irish time, just shy of a five-hour flight. We were unaware at the time that our tremendous tail winds were due to Hurricane Gustave.

Despite the toll that a west-to east transatlantic trip takes on the body, the adrenaline was running. We had visited Ireland frequently, but this was the first time we were planning to stay, and the excitement level was pretty high.

Mary's cousin, Martin Ryan, was there to greet us and escort us home, but because we had nine pieces of luggage and seventeen pieces of cargo, we decided to lock up the luggage, leave the seventeen pieces at Air Cargo, and go to Ryan's for tea. It was a beautiful but nippy morning.

Martin called a nephew, Derrick Burke, who agreed to meet us at the airport at 4:00, and then he drove us out to Lisnagry, the suburban area that was to become our new neighborhood.

On the way, we drove through the University and, after a quick stop at a convenience store (a new phenomenon in Ireland), we proceeded to our house, "Lauran."

I took a cab to the airport that afternoon and met Derrick at Customs. The officer fumbled around telling me we couldn't possibly get all the pieces cleared until tomorrow. When he saw Derrick (who works for Aer Lingus), he said, "Is he a relative?" Derrick answered "yes," the man disappeared, and amazingly, in five minutes, returned with my papers all stamped. They had ritually cut open two boxes and rewrapped them with Customs tape. It's not what you know...

I called Mom that night to inform her of our safe arrival. She told me that Father Jack Morse, who was one of my/our dearest friends, had died that morning. We had tried to see him before we left, but the hospital authorities wouldn't let us in. It broke my heart.

He had married us and had come to Washington, D.C., to be with us when Kate was hovering between life and death.

Kate was a preemie born at seven months, weighing only three pounds. She spent the first five weeks of her life in the Intensive Care Nursery of George Washington Hospital, in Washington, D.C. Father Morse later baptized her, and when she was eight, he celebrated a private First Communion Mass for her. In between, and since, he and Father Leo Wimett were regular visitors at our home.

It was a hell of a way to start our new venture in Ireland.

Wednesday, September 5. We spent most of the day unpacking and sorting. I called the University to let them know I had arrived and then decided to go in and look around. Kate came with me. We met Prof. T. Henry Ellis who heads the European Integration Department and who had a daughter in Kate's new school (Villiers). I also met Dr. Paddy Doran, the Dean of the College of Humanities, who comes across as a delightfully witty, if somewhat potty professorial type; Professor David Coombes, the resident authority on European Integration, Fionnuala MacMahon, who is the factotum in the Humanities School and John Stapleton, with whom I hit it off immediately. Stapleton has a roguish Kilkenny wit and one of the greatest commands of the language I've heard in years. He earned his Master's Degree in Public Administration at Albany State in New York.

I also made it a point to see Dr. Ed Walsh, the President, who had extended the invitation to teach here but who appeared to be absolutely taken aback when I walked into his office.

"John, how good to see you. Are you visiting Ireland?"

"Yes. For the rest of the school year."

Next I went to the reception desk where the telephone and fax boards are located. I always like to know the folks at the nerve center of any operation.

One of the curious things I noticed was that everyone seemed to call everyone else by his/her first name. Even the secretaries called Dr. Doran, "Paddy," and most people called the President, "Ed." None of the intellectual elitism I have found on other campuses.

Kate and I went over to the Parkway Shopping Centre (the only one in Limerick and minuscule compared to home). We had to stop the clerk periodically to subtotal our bill so we would know if we had enough money. Hadn't been to a bank yet and we were going through the pound notes pretty fast.

Thursday, September 6. Mary, Kate, and I took a cab in this morning. They got out at the bus stop in Castletroy (where the University is actually located) and took the bus into Limerick to Villiers. I went on to school and wandered around most of the day "meeting and greeting."

That afternoon our next-door neighbor, Peter Rolls, came over. He's in the process of building a house and hopes to be in by mid-November, although someone told me that the crew working on the house actually took the month of August off because the weather was so good! There certainly is a laid-back attitude around here.

Friday, September 7. I went into school this morning for a prearranged meeting with John Stapleton. He is a fascinating individual with a droll wit and the makings of an absent-minded professor (although he's only in his early forties.) I thought how strange it was that we might have met fifteen years ago if I had gone to Albany after Hugh Carey's election as Governor of New York.

Malachy Glynn, the CEO of the University's Foundation, called to ask if Mary, Kate and I would join him and his wife Betty for dinner. Malachy is the fellow who originally contacted me about helping the University with a little problem in Washington. In a sense, then, he is the unwitting midwife to my new venture. I said we'd be happy to go (even though I had just leased a Hertz car for the weekend).

The girl from Hertz brought the car out to the University and then asked if I would drop her off at a Ford dealer just down the Dublin Road from School. Off we went. When she got out of the car, I suddenly realized that I was sitting behind the wheel of a stick shift with everything (steering wheel, controls, etc.) on the "wrong" side. After several stalls, chugs, and jerks from the car, and hilarious outbursts from the lads in the garage, I got it running. Made it home without any serious trouble, although I hadn't driven legitimately on the left hand side of the road for about five years.

Malachy and Betty picked us up around 7:00 and we headed north to Killaloe on Lough Derg in East Clare. Dinner was at a quiet little place called the Lantern Lodge. The restaurant overlooked the lake and an incredibly beautiful valley. The food, the ambiance, and the company couldn't have been more enjoyable. We talked about everything and Kate, who was twelve, was very sophisticated. She even joined in the storytelling. I almost burst my buttons when she began to share anecdotes like a thirty-year-old.

Saturday, September 8. I drove over to the Village of Castleconnell about three miles from the house to pick up a phone directory. The postman had tried to deliver it yesterday.

When I returned, we left for Martin and Betty Ryan's. They live in Newmarket-on-Fergus over in County Clare, about twenty miles away. Their daughter and son-in-law, Barbara and Frank Shalloo, and a slew of kids were there. The conversation was very sophisticated and literate. Betty had been a teacher in her youth, Barbara is a school principal and Frank teaches at the Ard Scoil Ris run by the Irish Christian Brothers. They are all well traveled and politically active (Fianna Fail Party) people. The conversation was supplemented by hot tea, scones, and a roaring turf fire.

We decided to go on to the open market in Ennis. It was colorful and earthy, with sheep, cattle, and goats being herded right through the streets. Vendors shouted out their wares and farmers were horse-trading all over the place. For a few minutes at least, we had stepped back into an uncomplicated, bygone era.

I needed a hammer and a monkey wrench for some odd jobs around the house and thought maybe I could get a deal at the market. The wrenches were all made in China. So much for the simple, rural, isolated farm town!

Mary had packed a picnic lunch, so we continued on northwest up to Lahinch on the Atlantic shore. There is a spectacular view from the village, both north toward the Cliffs of Moher and south along the lower coast strewn with the shattered remnants of once-great cliffs. It was a terrific beach day. We ate on the rocks and then walked the sandy beach—it was low tide and the beach was probably seven hundred and fifty feet deep.

There were about seventy-five to one hundred people at the water's edge with rubber rafts, kayaks, and various diving gear. Kate and Mary were sunning themselves, so I wandered over toward the crowd. As I got close, two men dragged a third up on the beach. They started CPR and mouth-to-mouth resuscitation. I called excitedly to the girls to come over, and then stood staring at the kid who had been pulled up. He appeared to be about seventeen or eighteen. He was bluish and looked stone-cold dead. One of the rescuers shouted, "No pulse!" with a funereal finality.

Within seconds, he called out, "Pulse!" and with that, the "body" jumped up to great cheers. It had been an end-of-the-season competition by the lifeguards and this trio had just won. By then, I had practically turned blue myself.

We drove on up the couple miles to the mind-boggling Cliffs of Moher. Sheer rock shooting eight hundred feet out of the ocean with gushes of spray that drench the spectators at the top. The Aran Isles were as clear as could be, and we could see all the way up across Galway Bay to the taller peaks of the Bens. It was fabulous.

Sunday, September 9. I ventured out on the Limerick-Dublin Road on my bicycle for the first time this morning. Rode to a newsstand/shop. The clerk seemed very knowledgeable about what goes on at the University. I'm not sure whether it's local pride, curiosity, or simply the small size of the community.

We all loafed during the morning. The weather was still gorgeous. Finally, we went to the 12:30 Mass at Monaleen Church. Most people around here don't even know the "names" of the churches. Churches are simply identified by their locations, and Monaleen is the settlement between Lisnagry and Castletroy. (The technical name of the Church, I learned, is St. Mary Magdalene.)

During the middle of Mass, two dogs walked into the church, wandered up and down the center aisle, sniffed the place out, and left nonchalantly. No one in the congregation or on the altar even missed a beat. Dogs are everywhere and are practically considered family. As a matter I fact, I have noticed that the people seem very close to nature here—to the earth and the animals.

We came home, changed clothes, and then took off along the Cappamore Road, which winds through the foothills in County Tipperary. Went through some absolutely beautiful landscape and villages (seemingly untouched for centuries). Lots of one-lane roads with hairpin turns. It's a real challenge driving with one eye on the road, and one in the rearview mirror while the pilot, co-pilot, and navigator are all rubbernecking.

Kate had made up some sandwiches, so we had a quick snack in the car.

We stopped at the Dundrum House not too far from the village of Cashel. (Cashel, of course, is my family's ancestral home.) We had stayed at the Dundrum House a few years back, and it was still as peaceful and elegant as we'd remembered it. As we drove down toward Tipperary town, the Galty Mountains in the background set off the beautiful rolling hills and the Glen of Aherlow.

We came back on the Waterford-Limerick Road and decided to check out the Ahane Church at the end of Clyduff Road (our street). It is actually our parish. The church is in a serene, bucolic setting. At one time, Ahane was probably a bustling little village, but now there was only the church, a few houses, no shops and not even a pub!

Monday, September 10. Up early to take Kate to school, return the rental car, and hop a bus back to the University.

After lunch, I went for a walk along the River Shannon, which flows right beside the University. The pathway was incredible. Within four minutes of the main buildings, I was completely cut off from the rest of the world. There wasn't a modern sound to be heard—just rushing, gurgling water, blue herons

3

diving for fish, the wind in the cattails, the flutter of white swans and a variety of avifauna. I felt transported.

When I got back up to the Humanities office, I found a note that Paddy Doran was looking for me. I went down to his office and we spent about an hour together discussing some of the dimensions of my involvement here. He's a very open and likeable man, scholarly without being pedantic.

Late that afternoon, Mary and I met Dierdre and Pat O'Sullivan, our next-door neighbors on the other side. He's with the Customs office at Shannon. They're a very nice couple with two sons, Donn and Eoin, aged, I would guess, about ten and thirteen respectively. They offered to be of any help they could. I'm sure we will be taking them up on that.

Tuesday, September 11. Rather unexciting day. I went in to school and spent the entire time researching and writing in preparation for my lectures. Came home fairly drained mentally. I felt great, however.

Wednesday, September 12. I rode my bike in to school for the first time today. It's about a twenty-minute jaunt (two and one half miles). It was a pleasant day, but a little scary in all that traffic. There are no real shoulders, so I had to negotiate the outer ridge of the pavement and dodge cars at the same time.

Met with the professional staff of the Library and found them most helpful, even though their resources are painfully limited.

There was a reception in the Administration Building (Plassey House) in the afternoon. It was held to welcome the new faculty members.

Thursday, September 13. I rode to school again today—this time a little more confidently. Most of the day was spent reading and writing, although I also managed to check out several of the ancillary facilities—the Bank of Ireland, dry-cleaners, bookstore, etc.

Friday, September 14. This was Conferring (Graduation) Day at the University. The students finish their exams at the end of June, but do not actually graduate until the fall. Nothing works very fast in Ireland!

John Stapleton and I went over together to be gowned and hooded. My regalia consisted of a black robe with a gold and purple hood (government). It was my first academic processional (other than as a student thirty years ago). The colors were magnificent—like some medieval street show. Of course I felt like a piece of beef on the hoof, with everyone staring at me.

Over seven hundred students received degrees.

I met many of the faculty for the first time. One fellow, Dr. Nabil Adawy, is an Egyptian specializing in Middle Eastern geopolitics. He predicts there will be a war in the area and that it will more than likely involve poison gas. If it is quick, he thinks an area-wide war can be avoided. If it is protracted, however, it will spread and be bloody as hell. Time will tell.

Malachy Glynn sought me out after the ceremonies to have lunch with the University Board. It seems that Elizabeth Shannon (a Board Member and the widow of former Ambassador Bill Shannon) had raised a question about an American Studies program. When someone said there wasn't one, Malachy had chimed in, "Oh, yes there is—Mahoney is handling that."

I had a nice chat with Liz and told her that I had known her husband fairly well when he was with the New York Times' Washington Bureau.

During the lunch, I discussed the possibility of a full-scale American Studies agenda with the Foundation Chairman, Jim O'Connor, from Manhasset, Long Island, and Jack Daly, the Chairman of the Board of the University. Both expressed enthusiasm.

Saturday, September 15. As I was sitting in the kitchen this morning, the backyard looked particularly bucolic. We have had warm, pleasant weather for over a week now, and today the field behind the house was full of cows, pheasant, daws and other indigenous birds, and horses. The grass and the foliage are still lush in varying shades of green.

Pat Ellis, Henry's wife stopped over. She is charming, poised and sophisticated. The Ellises are devout members of the Church of Ireland, obviously raised in an Anglo-Irish tradition. They have a very matter-of-fact approach to life, fairly untypical of the Irish, at least from what I've been able to gather so far.

I tried my hand in the evening at making a fire in the sitting room (den) but I should have consulted my Boy Scout Manual beforehand. After several starts, I got a few flickers, but by then the ladies of the house were fast asleep.

Sunday, September 16. We walked to Mass at Ahane this morning and got swallowed up in the verdant environment. Our street becomes a country lane about a thousand feet from the house, complete with pastures, horses, asses, cows, chickens, and a riot of berries and wild flowers.

The church itself and the congregation remind me of the images I have of Pompey, New York (where my mother was born), of fifty to seventy-five years ago: people walking to Mass from all directions; an old Irish priest haranguing the membership with visions of hellfire and damnation; wizened, sunbaked men in their one suit; and a collection basket filled with small coins.

There were also, of course, the usual bunch of teenage boys and very old men who stood outside the church until the last minute, and when Mass had started, lumbered up into the choir loft or stood in the back of the church, shifting from one leg to the other—totally bored, but suffering through the obligation to be "physically present."

After Mass, we started back home and Mary pulled a plastic bag out of her pocket. There were a million blackberry bushes, and at least a billion blackberries en route. We picked and picked. We also ate and ate and nibbled black currants that grew by the bushel, as well as thorn apples, which would probably make great pies. The flowers along the roadside were beautiful. Fuchsia abounded and the gardens of the cottages along the lane looked like kaleidoscopes—there were so many colors and patterns. It took us an hour and a half to walk the one mile home.

Monday, September 17. I biked into school this morning and spent an hour with Patti Punch, the Deputy Librarian. She is a walking encyclopedia enveloped in a tornado. She is also part of an incredible information network, both locally and nationally.

Mary O'Brien, my godsend in the Departmental office, put me on to Eamonn Sheahan, a fellow in the print shop who dabbles in car sales. I have been following the newspapers for used cars since we arrived. For some reason, new cars are enormously expensive in Ireland. The smallest puddle-jumper costs anywhere from fifteen to twenty thousand dollars, and a decent car of moderate size is anywhere from twenty to forty-five thousand dollars.

Eamonn said he could get a car for me—one that could be brought back at the end of the year, for about sixteen to seventeen hundred dollars. Said it would be a "banger," a clunker, but "It'll get you from A to B."

The insurance problem I had anticipated apparently will not materialize. Hopefully, we can get wheels soon. Now if I can only afford the petrol—five dollars and seventy-five cents a gallon!

I saw a picture of Professor Noel Mulcahy in the Limerick Leader today. He was attending a meeting of the Fianna Fail Party. He's the Dean of the College of Engineering. I must get to know him better.

Peter Rolls, our neighbor, still claims he will be in his house within two months, although the pace of work is snail-like. In fact, no one has even showed up this week. I think it might have something to do with the hurling and football finals held on Sunday.

Tuesday, September 18. I biked into school this morning. It was cold and threatened to rain. There was a thirty-mile-an-hour headwind blowing in from the west (off the Atlantic). My bike almost stopped dead on the road two or three times. It was quite an experience with cars passing me at sixty miles an hour. I pumped, but nothing seemed to be happening. I felt for a moment like one of those high-wire bicycle acts that sits for what appears to be an eternity, fifty to seventy-five feet in the air, and then miraculously starts moving again. I did the same thing. How I managed to keep the bike upright still puzzles me.

I had a bowl of "Irish soup" in the cafeteria. It was tasty, but the consistency of the soup makes me think of the mystery dishes we used to get in college. It's opaque, watery, and tastes like it's seasoned with the same stuff bicycle shops use to repair inner tubes.

Kate came to my office from a field trip to Thomond College (directly adjacent to the University). She had her backpack with her. The poor kid had to lug that thing around because her school hasn't come up with a locker for her yet. We lashed it on to my bike, but of course I wouldn't let her ride the bike on the Dublin Road, and I wouldn't ride and let her walk, so we both walked, wheeling the bike. That was a real treat at 5:30 in the afternoon!

Wednesday, September 19. I rode in to school again this morning. The west winds were still pretty strong. They had reached gale proportions offshore last night.

After a few phone calls and some odds and ends, I went to a briefing/seminar for new faculty members.

When the formal presentations were over, we broke into small groups to do micro-lectures—on video. My stomach twisted in knots as I tried to figure out what I was going to say, how I should begin, who I was, where I was—and why was I born? Fortunately, it was only momentary. As a matter of fact, by the time we convened our mini-class, I volunteered as the guinea pig, and went on without a note. The Director of our session said afterward that mine was an excellent performance. He wanted to know how long I had been teaching. The others in our group were quite warm in their reactions, too. It made me feel as much at home as anything that has happened to me so far. Now, if I can add substance to style...

Eamonn Sheahan and I went out to look at a car and stopped at his house along the way. He invited me in to meet "the mother" and to see the renovations on their two hundred-year-old cottage. The place is situated in a gorgeous location overlooking Loch Gur and several Bronze Age ruins. I would guess we were about fifteen miles southwest of Limerick.

I expected to find a stooped old lady in a shawl—we had arrived unannounced. When we got out of the car, however, the first thing I spotted was a satellite dish, and then "the mother" met us at the door in a brightly colored print dress and a maroon sweater. Her hair had a permanent. She was smoking a cigarette. And she was in her eighties. The television was on in the kitchen (where everyone seems to gather in Ireland—and in Irish-American homes as well).

"Ye'll have some tea and biscuits?"

"Of course, of course."

It seems as though every time I turn around someone here is pouring tea and shoveling a biscuit into me.

We had a very sophisticated conversation about the Middle East, the United States, prices, etc. They watch CBS Evening News every night.

It was a wonderful visit.

Eamonn and I then headed for John Wrenn's house. John, who deals in used cars, lived "just down the road"—about eight miles, thirty-five turns, fifty bends in the road, two shebeens and four pubs "down the road." I think we even crossed a field somewhere along the way.

The area appeared bucolic, but every now and then, either between, or out from behind some trees, or shrubs, or walls, there loomed a restored Georgian country manor or an ersatz French chateau owned by a wealthy Continental or American.

John Wrenn's house is very modern, but, typically, the surroundings are a mixture of the sublime and the ridiculous. In the back there is a flowered meadow leading to his wife Margaret's parents' farm—and on the other side, hard beside the house, is a junkyard and garage with about fifty cars in varying degrees of disarray and damage.

John was a very pleasant guy and quite engaging. I offered him one thousand and fifty pounds for a car and he countered with one thousand and one hundred (a difference of about eighty dollars). We took the car out for a drive. It ran well but needed a sealant around the windscreen (windshield). I accepted his counter-offer and gave him a down payment of two hundred and fifty pounds. He agreed to fix up some minor items plus the sealant and to send the papers in to the County Council the next day. The system here is fairly bureaucratic, but exactly how full of red tape, I had yet to learn. The Council office apparently had to shuffle the papers and then send them back to me. I had to arrange insurance (about two hundred pounds) and then take the papers and the insurance policy back to the Council, who then issued a certificate which authorized the Garda Siochana (police) to grant me a window sticker. Eamonn drove me back home.

Thursday, September 20. I went to the personnel office today to work out some immigration matters, since we are still operating under three-month visas. Although I couldn't get all the right people together, there doesn't seem to be a big hassle over the matter.

Ann Smyth is the Deputy Director of Personnel and is a fascinating woman. I spent almost two hours with her discussing the "situation" in the North of Ireland. Literate, sophisticated, and knowledgeable, she was a nun for many years (she lived in the States for sixteen years). She was a native of Belfast and returned there in the early '70s. The horror stories she told about personal experiences, the people she knew (knows) who are or were involved in the conflict, the assassinations, the knee-capping (where persons suspected of treachery have their kneecaps shot off—rendering them crippled), the "Xs" on the doors, the psychological melodrama played out before her very eyes were totally absorbing for me. She did not romanticize or hyperbolize. It was tough, straight stuff.

After dinner, Mary, Kate, and I went for a walk. As we passed a meadow, I mooed and attracted a whole herd of cows and bulls, to Kate's delight. She got mad, however, when I wouldn't egg on the bulls to come closer. She's never seen an enraged bull.

At one point along the way, Kate was walking with a dog in her arms, while an old, lame, and I think, blind Terrier and two other dogs licked at her heels. She stopped and talked with a black cat and a Cheshire squatting on a wall, as well as three horses in two pastures. This all took place about two hundred yards from our house.

Friday, September 21. The temperature dropped dramatically last night—down to eight degrees Celsius—and the windows steamed up even though we had no heat on in the house.

I rode in to school wearing a sport coat, sweater, and beret—very continental!

Called Patti Punch for lunch, and she came by with some materials for my research. She took me on a tour of Thomond College after lunch. We must have met fifty people—and, typically, had a conversation with every one of them.

John Wrenn called. The car was ready and he had sent the transfer papers in to the Council. They must now stamp them and send them on to me.

I got thoroughly soaked riding home—a first—but my clothes were dry by the time I reached the house.

Brian Hanrahan, Sr. stopped in after dinner and brought two dining room chairs to make a full set. (We are leasing from his son and daughter-in-law.) Of course, he stayed for tea. He's a very interesting character, and I haven't met many dull ones yet.

He had been a professional football player and then played amateur until he was fifty. He has been in the catering and hotel business for a number of years and spent a good bit of time in the States. An engaging individual, he is a life-long Pioneer (non-drinker).

There had been an interesting coincidence during the day—another one. The lady at the insurance office asked where she should mail our papers. When I responded "Lauran," she said:

"Oh, you're living in Brian and Loretta Hanrahan's place. We live in one of their houses as well."

This is a very small place. There aren't many secrets.

Saturday, September 22. It was a gloomy, overcast morning. Kate had a friend over from school and during the course of the day, someone mentioned the Castle Oaks Hotel over in Castelconnell. Our young guest said her uncle used to own it.

I said, "What a coincidence. We had a visitor last night who also owned it at one time—Brian Hanrahan."

She said he was her uncle!

Mary and I went for a walk and stopped at an old house to admire the garden. There was a legend, "Beech Cottage," over the front door. An elderly man came out when he saw us. He had a round, cherubic face and pure white hair. His name was Tommy McNamara and this had been his home all his life. His brother Willy was visiting him and the four of us fell to discussing the twelve or fifteen varieties of flowers growing in the garden—fuchsia, Chinese lanterns, mums, roses, zinnias, and at least a half dozen others of which I had never seen or heard.

Eventually, we got around to talking about the neighborhood, which had been pure "country" up until just a few years ago. I asked about "fairy forts," which go deep into Irish legend. They are sacred, almost mystical circular mounds that strange folk used to inhabit. To the country people, they were strictly off-limits. God only knows what might happen if anyone set foot inside one.

Tommy and Willy said there was a fort down a boreen (a narrow road leading into a field or pasture) not too far away, but they did not encourage us to go there. We headed off anyway, took a farm lane, wandered around an abandoned nineteenth century farmyard, but could not find a ring mound, which we figured was by now covered with trees. We did find a wide variety of oak and cedar trees and carrot-like vegetation. It was very serene. But no fairy fort.

I had heard a story about the time Shannon Development Corporation wanted to bulldoze a fairy fort to construct a plant. The country people were so upset and put up such a fight that the authorities built the plant around the sacred site.

I had also heard an apocryphal but humorous tale of the woman who, when asked if she believed in the little people, replied, "No. But I've seen them."

Late in the afternoon, it cleared up and I suggested that we go for a bike ride to see if we could locate the confluence of the Mulcair and Shannon Rivers. The Mulcair flows about a half a mile from our house. We couldn't get there on bikes and we weren't wearing wellies (calf-length rubber boots named for the Duke of Wellington), so we couldn't walk.

We came back to the little village of Anacotty, about a mile from home, and rode the Mount Shannon Road. The Mount Shannon is two lanes wide, and from there we turned onto a one-lane road, then into a dirt/stone lane, and finally into a cow path. It might have been the most serene place we've found yet. Gorgeous vistas, stiff breezes, sunshine, and no sound other than an occasional cow. We got hit with a brief "misting" and then there loomed halfway across the sky a beautiful rainbow. The place, the moment, the scenery all came together—Ireland!

Sunday, September 23. We walked to Mass this morning. It was quite cold. In an effort to "get with it" sartorially, I wore a button-down shirt, a blue sweater and sport coat, charcoal slacks, dark loafers, a red, white, and blue regimental tie—and green socks. Everyone has heard of the Doors of Dublin, but not many know about the Socks of Ireland. It is not uncommon here to see business or professional men wearing black or gray pinstriped suits, matching shoes and ties—and white or orange socks. It's a bit of a culture shock.

After Mass, a young girl from across the street, Debbie O'Sullivan, came over. There are at least three O'Sullivan families in the neighborhood—all unrelated.

Kate and Debbie walked about two miles up the railroad tracks that run not too far from us. They went to an Irish version of a video game spot. We were apprehensive, but Kate is beginning to assert at least semi-independence. Anyway, Mary and I rode up to the place on our bikes but didn't go in. Kate ignored us when she came out. She wasn't too taken with the place, thank God. She walked back alone (with some dog she had found, of course). Fortunately, there are only about two trains a day on those tracks and they're not like real trains. More like Toonerville Trolleys—an engine and one or two small passenger cars.

Monday, September 24. School opened today and I have a hundred things to do this week.

It was very cold this morning. I could see my breath in the bathroom. Have to order some fuel today. The heat was turned on in my office, but even with that it couldn't have been more than fifty-five degrees Fahrenheit.

I stuck my head in the door to introduce myself to two colleagues on the corridor, Nick Rees and John Coakley, and then went to my office to write. I understand Rees did his M.A. at the University of South Carolina, so we will have at least an American connection in common.

Tuesday, September 25. There was little movement on the academic front for me today. Paddy Doran is leaving for the States next week; I don't know where Henry Ellis, our Department Head, is; Professor David Coombes is away until next week; Nick Rees is here today, but gone tomorrow. John Coakley is here tomorrow, but gone the rest of the week; and John Stapleton is off at a conference somewhere on the Continent. Oh, well.

Dr. Nabil Adawy stopped me today and we had an interesting conversation about not getting students too deeply immersed too soon. It was a very "meaty" talk, which I took to heart. I am rethinking my lectures now, to make them easier on both the students and me. I am also re-reading Daniel Boorstin's "The American Experience."

Coal, turf, and oil arrived today. The first two were reasonably inexpensive—about one hundred dollars. The oil was almost seven hundred dollars, but should last most of the winter. Jerry Connell, a neighbor from down the road a bit, stopped by around 8:30 in the evening. He had a truckload of fuel, four big bags of cut firewood and cut turf. He is a country lad from County Cavan. His sense of hospitality is genuine and it shows.

Wednesday, September 26. This was a fascinating and productive day.

I went to a seminar sponsored by the Irish Peace Institute. John Coakley came by my office and invited me. A Russian academic specialist spoke to about ten of us. He was very insightful. He talked about the internal problems confronting Mikhail Gorbachev, the history of "internal colonialism" within the USSR, the disintegration of the empire, and the gradual emergence of some sort of loose federation. He expects Ukraine, Byelorussia, and the Baltic States to have their own foreign policies within a couple years.

In the late afternoon, Eamonn Sheahan gave me a ride to John Wrenn's house. I had picked up the insurance and tax certificate earlier. We checked the car out (it ran) and I paid the balance. Margaret gave me a "luck penny," an old tradition in the country of rebating after a price has been agreed on. It was ten pounds. A nice personal touch.

Kate gave me the "throw up" sign when I pulled in the driveway. She hates the color (robin's egg blue) and isn't used to riding around in a clunker. After all those years in air conditioned Broughams and nine-passenger station wagons, this will do her soul good!

Thursday, September 27. We had our first frost of the season last night. There was a clear pink and cerulean Southern sky as I sat in the kitchen over coffee at dawn.

I drove Kate up to the Dublin Road to catch her bus. We have been walking up each morning, but today she was dragging. She didn't want to be seen in the blue (and used) car. I stopped around the corner from the bus stop and she got out. She was wearing long underwear—legs down to her ankles—exposed from the skirt to the red socks.

I hollered at her, "You're embarrassed to be seen in this car, but it doesn't even bother you to dress like that?"

9

She huffed back to the car, climbed into the back seat, pulled the long johns off over her shoes and socks, and stormed back to the bus stop without saying a word. A most auspicious start to the day. How soon before she won't even want to be seen with me, let alone a used car?

Mary and I had a 10:30 appointment with Detective Keating of the Garda to arrange for extended visas. We only had the standard three-month visitors visas and needed papers till the end of next June.

The Garda handle almost every "police" detail in the country. They are in the Civil Service (though there is a unique Constitutional ban against their striking or engaging in any sort of industrial action), they are unarmed, and they are quietly efficient.

Keating reminded me of the men I used to know in the Post Office and other federal agencies at home when I was younger. Most were well educated and articulate. Many had college degrees, as he did. When the Depression hit, they took government jobs and eventually became secure in their positions and never left. This fellow was about sixty. He told us that when he got out of college, things were tough in Ireland, but he didn't want to emigrate. It had a familiar ring. In fact, so much that we have encountered here—the economy, the sense of personal safety, the social mores, the families, the openness, and the lack of total commercialism—remind me of the America I grew up in thirty-five to forty years ago. It is refreshing in many ways.

We had arrived at Keating's office about fifteen minutes early and he saw us right away. What we experienced in the next hour and a half was a treat most people would be happy to pay for—a history of ancient Ireland, her wars, her heroes, the Anglo-Irish relationship, the 1916 rising, the Civil War, Ireland's "neutrality," the situation in the North, contemporary Europe, etc., etc. The man was encyclopedic and his education classical. When we left, Mary said she thought I had been transported—Keating and I had traded anecdotes about the Caesarian campaigns, American politics, and Irish mythology.

We got the extensions.

We drove back to the University and I gave Mary a mini-tour. When we arrived at my office, two young men were standing somewhat sheepishly in the hallway.

One stepped forward gingerly and said, "Mr. Mahoney?"

"Yes," I said, "are you David Curtin?"

He introduced himself to Mary, and then his buddy, Sean Lynch from Long Island, did the rounds. David's father grew up in Mary's neighborhood in Syracuse, and I had learned last summer that he might be coming to Limerick. Nice kids. They will probably be in one of my courses.

I drove Mary home and than came back to the Peace Institute. The speaker was a Norwegian professor who specialized in conflicts—civil wars, ethnic wars, tribal wars, and religious wars. I had a wonderful talk with him afterward, along with Tom O'Donnell, the Chairman of the Irish Peace Institute. Tom is a former Member of the Irish Parliament, a former Member of the European Parliament, and a retired Fine Gael Party leader. During our conversation, I suggested the idea of convening, perhaps under U.N. auspices, a conference of multi-national corporations who, with specialists in the field, could identify and possibly head off future conflicts. My premise was that most wars, although there is never only one reason for them, are fueled and driven by economic privation—the empty belly theory. If companies could locate and predict hot spots, and invest some capital in plant and assembly work in those areas, it would be a wise move. The cost in taxes, lives, lost resources and time, during and after a war, are dramatically greater than any expenditures beforehand. They all suggested that I put some flesh on my proposal and pursue it. I shall.

After the reception, John Coakley came up to me and said, "You don't take pints, do you?" and then proceeded to invite me in to Flannery's Pub on St. Catherine St. for a few.

I declined—graciously I hope—but it bothered me because this is a part of the social fabric of the place. Coakley is a man with whom I will be working closely during the next year and, I am told, he does much of his research in pubs. We shall see.

Friday, September 28. I went to the 1:05 Mass at school and asked Gerry Myers (the Catholic chaplain) to have lunch with me. We talked about the Church in Ireland today. He noted the fact that most people don't go to Mass, don't receive the sacraments, have little or no use for the clergy, and pay absolutely no heed to the hierarchy—yet they are very conservative and quite spiritual in a moral sense. He said, for instance, that divorce, which is constitutionally banned, would probably never be recognized even by a popular referendum.

He was curious about the relationship of American Catholics to the hierarchy. I told him that by Irish standards, the American laity would be considered quite liberal, although, ironically, by comparison to many of our Bishops, we are generally pretty conservative. He found that fascinating—although he was generally familiar with many of the very progressive social pronunciamento of the Catholic Bishops' Conference.

Thirteen days ago, I asked the fellow who looks after our house for the owners if he could get me a ladder. He showed up with it tonight. It took seventeen days to get the dining room chairs. The lawn mower, the key to bleed the radiators, and the fellow who is going to plant the bushes and flowers still haven't arrived. After almost a month here, I am beginning to realize that clocks and calendars serve no functional purpose in Ireland. They are purely ornamental.

Saturday, September 29. I woke up with a beauty of a cold. Up and down all day.

Late in the afternoon, Mary asked me if I would take her out to try the car. We went over to the Anacotty Industrial Estate, which is practically vacant, but which has miles of side roads and parking lots. She got behind the wheel and for the first time in her life, drove a right-hand-drive-stick-shift-with-all-the-instruments-in-the-wrong-place-on-the-wrong-side-of-the-road Mazda. To my amazement, although we had a few narrow misses with lampposts, curbs and bushes, she did very well. For about an hour we practiced everything but parking. I think parking is probably a separate lesson in itself.

Sunday, September 30. I had a bad night, sleepwise. I was somewhere between a whirling dervish and a bouncing ball all night. Aside from being tired, however, I felt better than yesterday and my cold had eased up.

Today was a paperwork day—mostly notes and bills.

We went to the Jesuit Church in Limerick for 5:15 Mass and afterward took a long drive east along the Shannon toward Foynes, an old port town. We found a great pier on the south side of the River, opposite Shannon Airport. We could watch the planes, scan the Shannon and Fergus Rivers, see the Clare Hills in the distance and view the lowering tidal activity all at once. We took another scenic route home. I had no idea where we were exactly, but I was wearing my Lewis and Clark hat, so we made it back without incident.

Monday, October 1. This was not a banner day. Kate stomped off to school in a snit. The washing machine door broke. I went to school and got so engrossed in correspondence that I missed an appointment with the computer office people—so I can't use my machine yet. I missed Mass because I lost track of the time. And John Coakley came by to tell me he was not going to be teaching Politics 101 this year, so my shared lectures with him are now on hold. As a matter of fact, we don't even know at this point if there will be a freshman course this term. Our meeting was pleasant but not particularly productive.

It also rained all day.

Tuesday, October 2. Thanks to Nick Rees, he and I got together this morning with John Stapleton and Eoin O'Sullivan (yet another O'Sullivan) who will be teaching Politics 101. It was an excellent gathering. We not only socialized over coffee, we actually laid out the broad structure of my lectures in politics, public administration, and European Studies. Nick and John indicated that it was very likely that I would be invited to join them next semester in a trip to the European Commission in Brussels for a hands-on session.

11

My cousin, Gen. Paul Gorman, faxed me that he and his wife Ruth are arriving on the twelfth for the weekend. Paul is delivering a paper to a NATO session at Cambridge, so they plan to make a side trip to Ireland. We are quite close to them.

Wednesday, October 3. I called Paul and Ruth to confirm their arrival. They asked if we needed anything and I said yes—Orville Redenbacher Popcorn, Grape Nuts, Tang, and something else I can't remember.

Sounds crazy but none of those items is available in Ireland—along with Hebrew National Franks, Hersheys' Chocolate, and decent paper towels.

Eoin O'Sullivan came by the office to lay out a suggested format for the split Politics course. Eoin is a sharp young man. He's a graduate teacher, finishing up his M.A. at the University. He's bright, sassy, and full of stuff—and only twenty-three-years-old.

He treated me with great deference at first, but I told him that it was HIS course and that I was there to supplement and to put an American "spin" on the subject. I think we'll get on well. He's very engaged with the homeless, both as an academic (he's doing socio-political studies) and as an activist. We have a lot in common there.

When he learned I'd been involved in American politics for over thirty years, his eyes rolled. I think he thought I must have helped James Madison write the Constitution.

Thursday, October 4. I mentally tried to structure my first lecture this morning. The dimensions are pretty well worked out and my research is about completed, but it will take a good bit of work to flesh it out. I want to pull together as much anecdotal material as possible to supplement the rather dry factual accounts.

Dr. Joan Alterkruse stuck her head in the door to say hello. She's my next-door neighbor on the corridor. She's a physician by training and, I believe, is Dean of the Medical School at South Carolina. She is on sabbatical and up to her neck in Irish Peace Institute activities.

I ran into Patti Punch in the hall. We walked through the Library, and I stopped to talk with the gal at the desk as Patti disappeared. While we were chatting, an engineering student from Germany came up to enquire whether she might help him with a problem.

He had been given an industrial design assignment to ferret out all literature on an automatic butter-spreading device. At first, he thought they were putting him on (it sounded to me like one of those old tricks we did in Boy Scouts—sending the young kids out in search of a skyhook, a latrine leveler, and a tent stretcher). He realized, however, that the assignment was legitimate and he was lost. There was no information available in the Library, but he knew if such a machine existed, the Americans would have it. The problem was how to run it down by the time his report was due, in two weeks.

I offered to help and said I would make some calls to Washington to find out who manufactures the machine and to see if we could get some material faxed over. I didn't even get the kid's name, but I figured he would find me.

Mary went off to cooking school tonight. Kate and I had dinner and then I read to her for an hour and a half. It was all poetry—Frost, E.A. Robinson, T.A. Daly, Dickinson, Sandburg—complete with pathos, inflections, and animation. She sat enthralled the whole time, stopping me occasionally for explanations, then nodding approval. She particularly reveled in well-turned phrases or colorful metaphors and similes. It was one of our better evenings. I wish she could stay that age and learn at my feet (sigh) forever.

Friday, October 5. I was working on my notes in the office when someone knocked at the door. It was the German lad. He introduced himself, Joachim Deuse from Dortmund, an exchange student from the University of Dortmund. He was twenty-two-years-old and looked like a poster boy for the old Hitler Jugenbund—six foot two, spare, blonde, ramrod straight. He was most deferential, but I put him at ease and we talked about everything. That was somewhere around 10:30 or 11:00 and when I looked at my watch next it was almost 1:00. He laughed and said he had enjoyed himself so much he had "cut" his

11:00 and 12:00 classes—and could he come back again next week? I had called Washington and had a few things working for him.

That afternoon, two young girls and a young lad approached me and asked if I was the new American Professor. They had heard about me and wanted to talk. I was on my way to the cafeteria and invited them along. We sat and gassed until after 3:00. I'd almost forgotten how inquisitive the collegiate mind is.

Mary and I took Kate and Debbie O'Sullivan to see "Grease" in town. The 8:00 curtain went up on Irish time (8:20) and the entré acte ran likewise, so it was well after eleven when we got out of the theater.

Saturday, October 6. While Kate went off with some of the neighborhood kids, Mary and I drove up to Ballina in County Tipperary, about fifteen miles away. It is on the southeast side of Loch Derg across a bridge from Killaloe, which is in County Clare. The Shannon flows through Loch Derg and technically separates the two counties.

We drove north on the Tipperary side toward Nenagh. A few miles on, we decided to head up a side road into the Ara Mountains. As we worked our way upward, the two-lane road became one lane, and this soon gave way to two ruts separated by a row of weeds. It started to rain and the "road' looked like something out of John Ford's version of O'Flaherty's *The Quiet Man*—bleak, scary, and lonely. All of a sudden, we saw a car in a ditch about two feet from the edge of the mountain. As we rounded a bend, there was a farm machine trying to pull the car back. We talked with one of the towmen. He said the driver had had one too many. We gave the guy a wide berth as he passed us going down the hill.

We then proceeded to the "Graves of the Leinstermen," a lookout overseeing Loch Derg. It was misting, but we could see for miles. We couldn't find anything to indicate why the place was called "Graves of the Leinstermen," but there was a roadside sign with that legend.

It stopped raining and Mary and I got out of the car. With my penknife, we cut gorse (yellow blossoms with tough, prickly green foliage) and purple/pink heather. They make excellent table arrangements.

The road back was much different. It was clear and downhill and we could see probably twenty-five miles in three directions—patchwork fields, Loch Derg, small lakes, mountains, and a forest. There are very few forests in Ireland. For the most part, they were destroyed during the English occupation. The timber was used to construct the ships of the British Navy and the trees were never replaced. The government is now engaged in a vigorous reforestation program and is encouraging emigrants to underwrite memorial groves.

Sunday, October 7. We went to the Salesian Church adjacent to the University this morning. Mary wanted to check out Confirmation classes for Kate.

After Mass, we drove over to Lissycasey in West Clare to visit Mary's cousins, Bridget and Patrick Hehir. The family cottage is actually up in the bogland in an area called Boloughera. West Clare is weather-tough and not particularly pretty except along the Atlantic coastline.

It was the first time I could recall going to Boloughera when it didn't rain. We only got lost once, and then not badly. We missed the turnoff from the Ennis-Kilkee Road (it was unmarked) but recognized it on the second try.

We spotted two ladies walking, and although I think we could have found the place ourselves, we asked directions. They knew exactly where the cottage was. We had to drive about a mile on a one-lane road with two very deep ditches on either side, not more than a couple inches from the road itself. No cars could possibly pass. We prayed that we wouldn't be met by an oncoming car. Whoever the Patron Saint of Protection Against Ditches is, he/she was on the job.

Everyone was waiting at the end of the driveway when we arrived. The last time we were here, they were all sickly and woebegone. Today, Pat (who is eighty-five and Mary's father's first cousin) was spry and alert. His wife Bridget, who is seventy-five, was full of stuff, and the children and grandchildren were in great humor. We stayed almost four hours (or two meals). The only person missing was son Michael who was at the local matches, a Sunday ritual throughout Ireland.

As we were leaving, Bridget sprinkled us with some of the Easter Water that was still left, then picked us a large bouquet of Michaelmas daisies—lilac with yellow centers. To top it off, someone put a huge bag of hand cut turf in the trunk of the car. It was pure Irish country hospitality.

Monday, October 8. This was not a particularly busy day, but I did meet with Eoin O'Sullivan and the first year Politics class (250 of them). Eoin introduced me to the class and I spoke for about ten minutes. They were rapt and quiet, although they laughed a couple times—fortunately in all the right places. When I finished, they gave me a firm round of applause. I was a little taken aback.

I asked the girls in the office if that was a common practice in Irish classrooms and they said they'd never heard of it before.

Tuesday, October 9. I saw Eoin O'Sullivan this morning. He said he told the students he was offended that they had never given him applause when he finished a lecture. He's already had them for three classes. So yesterday when he finished, they applauded.

Kate told me today that she is having some problems in school. Two or three of her courses are almost repeats of last year. She is bored and frustrated. At my instruction, she talked with the teachers in question and they have assured her something can be worked out. I hope this isn't just another manifestation of the "no problem" syndrome that affects most of Irish society.

I just got a fax from the Food Equipment people in Washington. I will try to meet with Joachim Deuse as soon as possible.

Wednesday, October 10. This was a very busy day. I am trying to discipline my lecture writing.

David Coombes had a reception for his M.A. students. I think there are about fifteen of them. I'm going to be working with them later in the year, so he asked me to join them. One of the students was an American, Lloyd Melnik from Scarsdale. Seemed very bright, but very far to the right politically.

The group invited me go pub-crawling with them afterward, but I graciously declined.

Thursday, October 11. I worked on my lecture notes today and then got the print shop to run off 250 copies of the U.S. Constitution for my students. The American dimension to the library holdings is absolutely ludicrous. I couldn't find a respectable text or reference work that was less than seventeen-years-old. This means, of course, that for my classes on American political institutions, the students will have to rely solely on my notes and a copy of the Constitution itself. It puts a hell of a burden on me—and them.

John Coakley stuck his head in the door and invited me to join several faculty members for "pints" tonight. I agreed, but went home and had dinner first.

About 9:15 I drove in to Flannery's on Catherine Street. Eoin O'Sullivan was at the bar. I ordered a Guinness and we sat and talked for about an hour. One could have a shot a cannon off in the place. I wondered where Coakley and all the rest of them were. All of a sudden, about one hundred and fifty people materialized out of nowhere, and the place was wall-to-wall with patrons. This is one of the great social phenomena of Ireland. The crowd doesn't show up at a pub until about an hour before closing time (sometimes less) and then they scramble to see how many pints they can either drink or line up.

Around eleven thirty, we went, en masse, to a disco called Ted's. It was like being in the States thirty years ago. Strobe lights, light rock, beer (or porter), and an air of innocent abandon.

I met a lot of interesting people from the University. One fellow, Jim Deegan, is in international economics. He asked me to lecture his classes on the U. S. Budget process. Brian Faloon (his nickname is Faloonski because he speaks fluent Russian, Polish, Finnish, Estonian, and Hungarian—as well as, I might add, German, French, Italian and Portuguese). Aside from his own lectures in European politics, he co-chairs a History Seminar and asked me to become a participant.

Coakley asked me to go to Cork with him the weekend after next for the Political Studies Association of Ireland annual conference.

Altogether it was a pleasant and productive evening, and I got home safe and sober.

Friday, October 12. I checked around school this morning to follow up on some of last night's conversations and found that most of the participants hadn't shown up for one reason or another. I later learned that, although the venue changed, the party continued until 4:30.

I picked Kate up at school. She was standing in front of the school gate with her friends when I drove up. She was obviously embarrassed by the ugly car and her eyes told me to "move that pile of junk." We are pretty much on the same wavelength, so I caught her message and parked about a block down the street. To my amazement, she offered one of her friends a ride home. When our passenger got out, I kidded Kate about the matter. She denied my assumptions. Anyway, I thought it was funny, and I thought her change of heart was very mature.

We drove out to pick up Paul and Ruth Gorman who were flying over from Heathrow Airport in London.

Saturday, October 13. We had a big breakfast and then took off for the day. The back seat was a little crowded, but the weather was beautiful and the company delightful. We stopped off to look over the University and then started east along the Shannon toward Tarbert in County Kerry. The ferry service runs across the River from Tarbert to Kilrush in County Clare.

We drove about ten miles up to Kilkee, a beach resort town. I stopped in a local, Hickey's Lounge, to enquire where we might find information on church/heritage records. Paul and I have traced the Gormans/O'Gormans back to the Shannon estuary, but we have never seen any actual on-site documents. The lads in Hickey's said to go see Tom Haugh, the church sacristan and local barber, because he knew everything there was to know about the environs of Kilkee.

Haugh was having lunch when we found his place but said he'd meet us at the church in ten minutes. He made it in twenty. Not bad by Irish standards. The five of us joined him in the sacristy and went through all the available records. Lots of Gormans (no O'Gormans, strangely) but nothing we could identify. We got two leads on other parishes and then left.

We all agreed that Tom Haugh was built like, looked like, sounded like, walked like, and dressed like Barry Fitzgerald. He even had his cap brim turned up in front.

We drove up the coast road to Lahinch and then went on up to the Cliffs of Moher. The wind coming in off the ocean must have been sixty miles an hour. It was awesome and breathtaking. Perfect view of the Aran Isles with a windswept, swollen ocean in between. Paul and Ruth were exceptionally pleased to be there.

Despite the hour, we decided to drive through the raw rocks of the Burren. The area reminds one of the Badlands in the Dakotas and the Southwest—mystical, creepy, inspiring, and preternatural.

We turned south at Ballyvaughan, which is on the south side of Galway Bay, but we ended up on the wrong road. At one point, climbing up the hairpin almost at twilight, we stopped to look back. There was an incredible rock gulf behind us almost a mile down, and beyond it lay Galway Bay and at the eastern end of the Bay were Salt Hill, Claddagh and Galway City alive with amber arc lights. It was splendid—worth getting lost.

Sunday, October 14. Mary and Ruth did sausages and eggs and homemade scones and then we walked to Ahane for the 11:00 Mass. The sermon was circa 1950—be sure to genuflect all the way, hold your heads up smartly when you receive Communion, don't talk in church, etc. We all controlled ourselves admirably.

It began to rain, so we did a somewhat truncated tour of County Tipperary and then stopped off at a lovely restaurant in Castleconnell for dinner.

Monday, October 15. We were all up early. I took Ruth and Paul to the Airport about 7:00 and then went on to school where I spent almost the entire day writing. I took about an hour and a half off to meet with Nick Rees and work on my lectures for his European Integration course.

I stopped in the cafeteria and while I was there, Mary Robinson, the Labour Party candidate for president, came over to say hello. I've been very impressed with her. I think she could pull off a "sleeper" victory, although the numbers are against her. My guts tell me that the polls are wrong (they have Brian Lenihan running away with the race), and that she has far more residual strength than many perceive.

There are thousands of people (particularly women) who will vote for her but who won't say so before the election. I saw that phenomenon in the Kennedy-Nixon race.

Lenihan has the machinery, but unless his troops are organized and motivated they might not turn out for him. The Presidency in Ireland, of course, is mostly an honorific post.

Tuesday, October 16. I finished my notes for Thursday's lecture. I'm still a little apprehensive, although I do feel better having my factual material all organized.

We had quite a night. Kate is showing signs of adolescence—the privacy syndrome. She is hanging around with older kids and doesn't want us to become involved with those relationships. It's probably normal, but they are two years older and one has a sixteen-year-old brother, and more exposure to the street. I worry about Kate getting too involved and say so frequently, which tonight, precipitated a modest confrontation.

Wednesday, October 17. I rewrote my notes in final, clean form and gave them to Mary O'Brien and Anne McCarthy in the departmental office to type. Unfortunately, they didn't grasp some of the more sophisticated language and the typing never got finished. At this point I don't know if my notes run forty-five minutes or an hour and a half. (I kept waiting for someone to say, "No problem.")

The political science gang reiterated John Coakley's invitation to join them in Cork this weekend. It should be an interesting and helpful few days.

Thursday, October 18. I had an absolutely fitful night. I rolled on a spit. At one point, I was so hungry I actually got up and ate a bowl of Grape Nuts, courtesy of the Gormans.

The lecture itself was almost anti-climactic. The students were attentive and they hung on every syllable. One could hear a pin drop—and it's a big lecture theater with two hundred and fifty seats and no public address system.

The grapevine this afternoon indicated that Constitutional studies aren't that drab after all. Made me feel good. Unfortunately, I had enough material for two lectures, so I had had to break off about midpoint. I'll try to blend the remainder in with my next lecture.

Eoin O'Sullivan asked me in the afternoon to submit questions for the final Politics exam. I was pleasantly surprised. The University operates on a trimester system of twelve weeks each, so finals are only a little over a month away.

Friday, October 19. This morning was fairly uneventful. In the afternoon, Nick Rees, John Coakley, and I drove to Cork for the PSAI meeting.

I met an amazing array of characters at the conference. Politicians, political journalists, and TV commentators, as well as serious scholars and just plain political activists. Typically, there was a late evening of talk and debate.

Saturday, October 20. There were panel discussions all day long with many opportunities in between for individual chats. I met the only professional lobbyist in Dublin, Myles Tierney, and obviously, we hit it off very well. At dinner, I sat with Ellen Hazelcorn from Chicago who is a Ph.D. at Dublin Tech, an affiliated school of Trinity College. She invited me to lecture her students and I said I would.

We had another long night in the bar, this time complete with loud debates. Tim Pat Coogan who just wrote a biography of Michael Collins, one of the giants in the war with the Black and Tans, the Anglo-Irish War, the Treaty with England, and ultimately, the Civil War, went after a right-wing academic at our table. A few sparks flew, but the confrontation was mostly a series of magnificently articulate put-downs. I sensed the presence of Oscar Wilde's ghost in the room.

The songs (how else to end such an evening) were very Irish—some sentimental, some seditious. They asked me for a few American numbers. I did some George M. Cohan, which fell flat. No one knew or related to either the words or the music.

Sunday, October 21. There were a few panels this morning, then breakfast and a scramble to find a church.

Coakley was elected President of the Association. A nice honor.

I rode back with Nick Rees and we stopped at the Jesuit Church in Limerick and then went over to South's Pub in the next block. I called Mary. She was hesitant to come in to town. It was misty and dusky. I said I'd get someone to bring me home.

A few minutes later, Mary and Kate walked in. She had driven at night. A first!

Monday, October 22. I was terribly sick today. It felt like food poisoning or the flu. Couldn't eat, and hardly stirred out of bed.

Tuesday, October 23. Still sick, but I managed to get in to school. I had lunch with Malachy Glynn and we discussed some fund-raising angles for the University Foundation.

Wednesday, October 24. I felt a little better today, but not really well.

My old friend Beverly Knowles called me from Killarney. I've known her for thirty years. She was personal secretary to Senator Lee Metcalf of Montana for years. She was traveling with friends, knew they weren't going to get as far as Limerick, but didn't want to leave Ireland without calling.

Thursday, October 25. I saw posters announcing a visit to the campus today by Austin Currie, a Fine Gael Party member of Parliament and that Party's candidate for president. He was scheduled to speak at the same time as my lecture. I released the class and told them I'd see them in the lecture hall with Currie. Ha-ha. I imagine fifty percent of them went to the Canteen and another thirty percent went to the Stables Bar. Anyway, they had a chance to see him if they wanted.

Later in the day I went to a reception for the Irish-American Partnership, a group of American-Irish businessmen who were being whirled around the Island looking at "projects."

Friday, October 26. There were a dozen mechanical chores to handle today: collecting material for my European Integration lectures, sending a fax on the butter-spreader, getting professional cards printed, dropping off laundry, securing a list of the Partnership members from their Dublin office, several calls to the States, a meeting with John Stapleton on Public Administration, and a meeting with Willie O'Dea, the member of Parliament from Limerick who has invited us to a rally for Brian Lenihan tomorrow.

After dinner, Mary and I walked in to the Black Swan, the local in Annacotty. We just wanted to see who was there and to introduce ourselves. True to form, there was hardly a soul in the place when we arrived at 9:30.

At 10:30 the room was packed. It was the Irish "pub phenomenon" again. We went home a little after 11:00.

Saturday, October 27. I had a lot of paperwork to do in the morning and took a snooze in the afternoon. John and Margaret Stapleton had invited us to dinner tonight—not to arrive until 8:00. I biked in to Annacotty to pick up a jar of the local honey as a house gift.

Although it was drizzly and gloomy, we went to the Savoy Hotel in town to meet Brian Lenihan's campaign caravan. When he emerged from the coach, he spotted me on the sidewalk and shouted to me over the crowd "Mahoney!" in the proper Irish pronunciation of the name. Then he made a beeline for me and threw his arms around me. We chatted for a second and he turned to the newspaper people covering him and said:

"This man is the greatest lobbyist in Washington. He and I used to work together years ago. We didn't need anyone else. We didn't even need the President."

It was raw political hyperbole, but Kate's eyes got as big as saucers. I loved the whole show. Made me a bit nostalgic. Then he was off down the street, kissing babies and shaking hands.

I had gotten to know Brian quite well from his many visits to Washington over a twenty-five year period. Somehow or other, we always managed to end up at the same receptions or involved in the same issues. We first met when John W. McCormack was Speaker of the House of Representatives, in the 1960s.

Brian's cronies in the Fianna Fall Party fondly referred to him as "Bingo" because when there was a tough political job to do, the party leaders used to say, "Give it to Lenihan and, bingo, it'll be taken care of."

We arrived at Stapletons timely, which was early by Irish standards. They have two beautiful kids, Patrick, about seven, and Meghan, perhaps two.

Another couple, John and Phil Lovett, came about twenty minutes later (or right on time, if you will). John is the personnel manager for Krups, a German appliance and engineering company located locally. Phil owns a bookstore and is very involved in the women's movement. A fascinating couple.

We sat down for dinner around 9:30 and, as my Pop used to say, the conversation flowed as freely as the grace of God. John Lovett has as beautiful and colorful a command of the language as anyone I have met in a long time. Phil seems the knowing and sage mother, but not matronly. Margaret reminds me of the lead female role in Singe's *Playboy of the Western World* (I can't remember whether it was Maureen O'Hara or Siobhan McKenna who played it), and John Stapleton is the cunning, brilliant Kilkenny working-class intellectual.

It was an altogether refreshing night. We discussed at some length Irish politics, the Travelers (or Tinkers as they are sometimes known), Irish history, the North, the European Community, poetry, philosophy, modern literature. It was an Irish salon.

We left at 3:00 a.m. full of tips, ideas, new leads, and new friends.

Sunday, October 28. Everyone slept late this morning. Kate had gone with us last night, played with the kids early on, watched television later, and then fell asleep. The clocks were set back an hour today, however, so we didn't lose a whole lot of the day.

I biked in to Ryan's in Annacotty and picked up the newspapers. There are no papers delivered to homes here. It's too impersonal. It is very important to the Irish that they buy a paper <u>from someone.</u>

I took a nap in the afternoon and then we dressed and went in to the 5:15 Mass at the Jesuit church.

After dinner, Mary and I drove over to the Claughan GAA (Gaelic Athletic Assn.) Hall for a rock'n roll party—"music from the Sixties"—with Jim and Niamh O'Sullivan and Dierdre and Pat O'Sullivan.

It was the October Bank Holiday, so no one had to work Monday.

We danced our feet off. It was great. The DJ asked us to join the Rock 'n Roll Club and one of the regular couples asked us if we would join their group in the rock 'n roll dance contests upcoming. With our "jive" steps, their group would certainly win.

Monday, October 29. Although it was a holiday, I went in to school to write and to make some telephone calls. Not a soul around.

Tuesday, October 30. I had a funny experience in the Library this morning. A woman whom I had never seen came up to me and said, "I hear you're the John Travolta of Limerick." This town is too small to believe.

It poured much of the day—cold and windy. Irish winter weather, they tell me. I certainly hope we don't have to live with six months of this!

I went to get in the car late in the afternoon and the battery was dead. I pushed and pulled—thought I would drop dead in the parking lot—but my coordination was off. The front seat is small and I couldn't push the car and then jump in and engage the gears fast enough to "catch." It was very frustrating and I got drenched, with no umbrella and no hat. Three different students gave me a push -for about forty-five seconds each —and then disappeared.

Finally, a fellow in a jeep stopped. He had jumper cables. We got it going and I drove to the Black Swan to dry off. Couldn't help thinking of Robert Benchley's great line, "I've got to get out of these wet clothes and into a dry martini."

Only stayed for a few minutes, then ran home for a hot shower and dinner.

Wednesday, October 31. It was a rather tense day politically in Ireland, Brian Lenihan got sacked as Tanaiste (Deputy leader of Parliament) by the Taoiseach (Prime Minister) over a mysterious phone call to the President's office years ago. The call itself doesn't appear to be all that serious, but the matter has become a cause celebre because Lenihan at first denied making the call and then, when confronted with a taped interview several months ago in which he admitted the call, he changed his story. It was modestly reminiscent of Watergate, a stupid move, then a cover-up, then an exposure. I'm not sure what all the implications of this are, but the Prime Minister is not the most popular guy in Ireland and this could generate some sympathy for Brian.

I went to my first academic meeting today. It was a little tense. Essentially, as with all political gatherings, the tension was over turf—not the kind one burns, but the kind over which one rules. Sat through two and a half hours of it—silently—although I think I might have developed some thoughts for the next session.

Thursday, November 1. My lecture today was on the relationship between the three branches of the U.S. Government—the balance of power. I thought it was pretty good and fairly lively. A young girl in class turned green and then white about halfway through the hour. Then she went down. I had some kids hoist her into the aisle and I got down on my hands and knees to force her head down. Her color came back quickly, but she started to get sick so I got two hulks to carry her out and someone else to call the nurse.

I let the class calm down, said nothing for about three to four minutes, and then quietly resumed the lecture. It worked out okay.

During the course of the afternoon, there was a steady stream of students revolving in and out of the office. I felt like my old family physician, Dr. Bill Ryan, but it was great to see their interest and enthusiasm.

About 5:30 I stopped over at the Stables with Nick Rees, John Coakley, and Marie Kirwan, one of the workhorses in the Humanities School. That was a mistake.

Coakley offered to give me a ride home. I called Mary and said I was on my way. Then Coakley disappeared. He came back about two pints later, at which point we all left for Lisnagry.

We got almost to Annacotty, when Coakley said, "You have a real nice local here. I haven't been in it for a while. We should stop."

We stopped. Unknown to me, he had called more people who arrived shortly. By then it was time for the Presidential Debate. I called Mary again. They all left after the Debate and I said I would walk home. I fell to talking with a few of the regulars and the place closed. It was 11:00. One guy offered me a ride home. I didn't realize until I got outside that he was talking about a motorcycle. I was panic-stricken riding up the middle of the Dublin Road. Fortunately, we only had to go about five minutes. Mary was quite ticked. It was my first dido in many years.

Friday, November 2. I spent most of today researching for Nick's class on the 13th. Went home about 5:00. Early night—and rather chilly.

Saturday, November 3. I went over to school to use the Library but it was closed, so I spent a couple of hours writing my European Integration lecture.

We had an early dinner. Debbie O'Sullivan came to stay overnight. I asked Mary if she'd like to go in to the Black Swan. Said she'd love to. I suggested we invite our neighbor Martha Laffan. Martha, who is widowed, was delighted with the invitation, and so about 9:30 we picked her up and drove in. It was a fun evening. Just the three of us. Martha is great fun, well educated, articulate, and very witty. She said since her husband died, she doesn't get invited to social events that often. That is a painfully true commentary on Irish life and customs, I am told.

Sunday, November 4. We went to a children's Mass at the Salesian church with Kate and Debbie. I thought it was a disaster—and interminable!

Debbie left after breakfast and the three of us went for a long drive through County Tipperary (and parts of Wales, I think; we were so far afield). We finally wound around the foothills and reached Loch Gur, which was fascinating. It is a Mesolithic village site about ten to fifteen miles southwest of Limerick dating back to five thousand BC. We walked around for a while but decided the place was better visited when we could spend the entire day and do some serious climbing and exploring. There are circular stone formations away from the village site, which appear to have religious or astrologic implications (similar to Stonehenge). It's something we're anxious to probe further.

Monday, November 5. I wrote for an hour or so before leaving for school.

Father Haugh from the Village of Cross, in County Clare, called today. He was one of the people Tom Haugh from Kilkee had recommended as a possible lead in running down information on the Gorman clan. He had done some research on Patrick (Gorman) O'Gorman for me but came up with nothing. Patrick O'Gorman was my great-grandfather's name. We'll keep trying.

Tuesday, November 6. The papers are full of the Irish election. It's been a squeaker. Brian Lenihan has been up and down and belted from pillar to post. It appears that he will win the complicated preferential balloting in terms of a plurality, but because he won't get an absolute majority, the second preference for those who vote for Fine Gael (Austin Currie is barely in the race) will be counted. At that point, it is very likely that Mary Robinson will poll enough second preference votes to win. It's interesting for Ireland—a woman, a socialist, a supporter of divorce, and an advocate of abortion rights. Her campaign song was "Mrs. Robinson."

Wednesday, November 7. I heard on the radio this morning that Ann Richardson had won in Texas. The other news is sketchy, as we can't get American newspapers and we purposely don't have a television set.

Had a letter from Father Culligan in Carrigaholt over in Clare. He, too, had no luck on the Gorman/O'Gorman ancestors.

I talked with Bob O'Malley in the Doorkeepers' Office at the House of Representatives in Washington. He gave me a rundown on all the House and Senate races. All in all the results were pretty good, i.e., most of my friends had been re-elected. A couple of very effective, hard working members were defeated, however. It's one of the pities of the business that the guys who dedicate themselves to understanding and then solving problems, frequently forget to go home, and the public thinks they've gone high-hat and throws them out. It's part of the price we pay for a representative democracy.

Ireland is at the polls today.

Thursday, November 8. The vote counting started this morning. The result is still sort of "iffy."

I gave a lecture on Congress and the White House today. I thought it went exceptionally well. Very substantive. The class wrote furiously. Again a round of applause, a queue at the lectern after class, and another steady stream at my office. There's no business like show business...

Everyone gathered for an election analysis at the Stables late in the day. I asked Mary to come in. We eventually proceeded to the Lock Bar in town. Fun crowd and live traditional Irish music.

We went home fairly early since we still don't like to leave Kate alone for too long, although she has developed a pretty good social network in the neighborhood.

Friday, November 9. It was fairly quiet today, in spite of the variety of faculty and students in and out of my office. Nick Rees and I went over bits and pieces of next Tuesday's lecture on "External Influences on the European Community." It's my maiden voyage with this class.

It is official now. Mary Robinson was elected. She will be sworn in on December 3.

Mary picked me up at school. We had to "stick the cycle in the boot" (put my bike in the trunk), since I had ridden in to work.

Saturday, November 10. I took Kate out to Ashroe Riding Stables in Newport this morning over her forceful objections. Mary and I feel she is getting into the teenage "lounging and grazing" syndrome, doing nothing, with no exercise and no outside interests. She's only twelve and isn't ready for that stuff. She needs some structured activity yet.

I loved the horse they gave her—a chestnut named "Pride." Obviously gentle. Kate enjoyed herself, but even more important, she ran into a whole bunch of classmates. That's when her interest in the place began to soar.

Sunday, November 11. I completed the first draft of my lecture for Thursday.

Mary and I went in to a new church, officially St. Patrick's. It is a small fieldstone building on Clare Street in Limerick. Kate went to Ahane with the neighborhood kids.

Mary wanted to see "The Field" starring Richard Harris and John Hurd.

It was a good movie, very moving. There were all the elements of psychodrama and pathos and angst and ethnic pride. I hadn't seen anything by J.B. Keane on the screen, so it was a new experience. As prose, the movie left a little to be desired, but as poetry, it was superb.

Monday, November 12. I rewrote my lecture on European Integration for tomorrow—legibly, this time, so the girls could type it.

Tuesday, November 13. The lecture went well. About ninety students. Some of the material was bewildering to them. They didn't understand the structure of the U.S. Government, the powers of the three branches, or the role of lobbyists. I think I opened their eyes, however. They were attentive for the most part. Got a rousing ovation at the end, and several students crowded around the lectern.

I dropped in to see Paddy Doran regarding my American Studies proposal. He was quite effusive and asked me to pursue the matter. I was delighted, because I thought he would demur. He is hurt by the University's refusal to accept Humanities as an equal partner with Engineering and Business in the school's structure, and he feels it impairs his efforts to broaden the scope of the College. He was rather vocal on the subject.

Malachy Glynn asked me to intercede with Speaker Tom Foley as the headliner at the 300th anniversary of the Treaty of Limerick next year. It would be in memory of the "Wild Geese" who had to flee Ireland and the contributions they and their descendants and successors made around the world.

Wednesday, November 14. I spent most of the morning writing.

Mary came in around 12:00 and we went over to Plassey House for lunch with President Ed Walsh and his wife Stephanie, and Paddy and Hannah Doran. It was simple but very tasteful, and the conversation was warm and animated. Lots of serious talk. Lots of laughs. Mary and the Walshes then left for a ceremony marking the reconstruction of a Jewish cemetery here in Castletroy. There are only two Jewish families in the Limerick area now, both jewelers, although there was a thriving community here until an anti-Semitic outbreak in 1904. It was led by some half-baked Redemptorist priest. The local community dispersed. There are many Jews still in Ireland, however. Mary had a nice chat with the former Lord Mayor of Cork (Goldberg) and, of course, Dublin was led for years by Lord Mayor Briscoe who was also a Member of Parliament.

It was an ecumenical service, with all the headliners from the Roman Catholic Church, the Church of Ireland, and the Presbyterian and Methodist Churches.

I went to an all-Humanities faculty meeting, which lasted for five hours—a record. Lots of turf wars. It was quite fascinating to learn how courses and modules are constructed.

Thursday, November 15. Fiona Casey, one of my graduate students, asked me for my notes on the freshman Politics course. She is doing tutorials for the course and wants to get a handle on the material I've been covering.

I gave a lecture on pressure groups in general, and Washington lobbying in particular, today. Warm response and attentive note taking. I told them a personal lobbying anecdote about Congressman Fred Rooney on a critical vote in the House Commerce Committee a few years ago. They sat bug-eyed as I described the tension in the room that day and my anguish at not knowing whether he would vote for me or how the total vote would come out. When I told them that after all the drama, he had voted with me and that I had won the vote, the whole class burst into applause. We all laughed out loud. I think it went well.

Friday, November 16. I worked on my European Integration lecture for next Tuesday and generally kept busy all day.

Mary came in and picked me up. Kate had a house full of company. After dinner, we laid down the ground rules for the kids (everyone out by 10:30, Kate in bed by midnight) and then went in to some yuppie bar to meet Coakley, Nick Rees, and two recent acquaintances, Paul McCutcheon, a Law lecturer and Dr. Bernadette Whelan, who teaches History. We proceeded to the Aero Club at Hanratty's Hotel and stayed until 2:00 a.m. It's a sophisticated disco—a real kick. We danced a great deal and had some hilarious conversations about cricket, soccer and baseball. I, of course, assaulted and belittled cricket and defended baseball, and McCutchen, who plays cricket, did just the reverse. A very funny, witty, droll crowd. Mary enjoyed it immensely. It was especially relaxing knowing that Kate was completely safe in our neighborhood.

Saturday, November 17. I took Kate to her riding lesson this morning. I was nervous because they started her off trotting and she was completely at sea. I was afraid she'd panic and fall off. I gave her instructions each time she rode past me.

Finally, with tears in her eyes, she said, "Will you please stop talking to me."

I went outside and watched the jumpers for the duration.

Mary and I went up to Killaloe to a dinner party that night. It was at Phil and John Lovett's. In very Irish fashion (we're catching on) we arrived at 9:00 for a sit-down dinner.

Dinner was served around ten o'clock. Coffee and dessert around 1:00 a.m. When I next looked at my watch, it was 3:00! It was by far the best evening we had had out in Ireland. The conversation, which ranged from politics to Roman History, Irish History and literature, foreign affairs—you name it— was exciting. Senator Mary Jackman and her husband Nick were there, John and Margaret Stapleton, Dr. Dearbhil ni Cairtaigh from Thomond College and her husband Roderick (a Romance scholar), and, of course, our hosts. I learned more about the workings of the Irish government that night than I ever knew.

Mary Jackman is a member of the Fine Gael Party, but quite progressive. She is likely to become a TD in the House in the near future. (Unlike the United States, politicians in Ireland consider a move from the Senate to the House as a step up.)

We left about ten minutes to five, and were not the last to depart.

Sunday, November 18. This was obviously a slow day for us. Kate went to the 11:00 at Ahane with all the neighborhood kids, and we went to the 5:15 at the Jesuit Church.

Monday, November 19. I got up early this morning to write my next lecture. Actually wrote the whole thing in one sitting—but after a good deal of research and thought. I took it in to the girls early so they'd have time to type it. The computers were down and there wasn't a normal typewriter to be found anywhere.

Tuesday, November 20. The computers never really got going, so I had to hand-write the whole lecture. I finished the final copy and the overhead props at about 2:35 for a 3:00 class! There was some absenteeism (I'm told it is common about this point in the term) but it was still a good group. Very attentive for the most part. I lectured on American Federalism and let them draw their own comparisons and conclusions for European Community implications.

   During class, I noticed one young lady talking, yawning, woolgathering. Afterward, she had the temerity to come up and say she didn't understand. Could she get a copy of my notes? Having worked on them for days, my first inclination was to get mad. Instead, I got very Irish.

   "No problem," I said. "I'll leave a copy in the office."

   Of course, there is no copy, but I wouldn't say "no" to her—just let her hang.

   Henry Ellis approached me and asked if I would draft three new modules for American Studies. It might be as a result of my conversation with Paddy Doran. He asked me to work with Nick Rees. Nick, old hand that he is, was skeptical about the proposal.

   Met with Eoin O'Sullivan to discuss the marking procedures for the Politics class. I learned that each course has an external examiner, or assessor. Ours is Professor Mike Laver from University College Galway, whom I met in Cork. The Irish grading system, while still on an A, B, C basis, is much more liberal than the American approach. Almost anything close to a fifty is a "pass" here.

Wednesday, November 21. Mary started planning in earnest for the Thanksgiving Dinner today. We have invited all the American students at the University, I guess somewhere between ten and twenty kids. David Curtin and Sean Lynch are doing the head count for us.

   I spent some time with Nick Rees discussing Tuesday's lecture and talking about Henry Ellis' proposal on the three modules for American Studies. Nick's skepticism is rooted in the fact that he apparently has already drafted proposals on other subjects for Henry, which have gathered dust on the shelf. I'm determined not to let that happen since more and more students are stopping me each day to ask questions about the American system.

Thursday, November 22. Thanksgiving Day and no turkey. We had planned to have our dinner on this date originally, but between the class schedule and Ed and Stephanie Walsh's reception for new faculty and staff tonight, it wouldn't work. We'll do it Sunday.

   I finally got the head count. Twelve students, plus the three of us. It should be fun. I thought there would be more, but fifteen is still a good crowd around the table.

   Went out to Newport (Oakhampton House) to Walshes about 8:00. Kate wasn't invited, so we told her to read and finish her homework and we'd be home early.

   When we got there, everyone made a fuss over our holiday.

   "Sorry we don't have a turkey for you."

   " Sorry we broke up your family tonight," etc.

   Anyway we had a fun time.

   Oakhampton House was built in 1770 and later abandoned. Ed and Stephanie started from scratch and rebuilt it. He is one of the most amazing people I've ever met. He is a registered silversmith, a licensed engineer, an accomplished architect, a painter, an expert horseman, and a very talented classical violinist. His breadth of interest and capacity reminds me of Thomas Jefferson.

We met many, many new faculty during a very gracious evening.
It did not seem like twenty-seven years had elapsed since Dallas.

Friday, November 23. Checked in with the family in the States. I think Thanksgiving is probably the toughest holiday for an American away from home.

I had coffee with Jerry Cronin who runs the cooperative education placement program for the Humanities College. Like Patti Punch in the Library, Jerry is a font of useful information.

Saturday, November 24. I took Kate riding this morning. She got "Pride" again, and I told the Mullanes (Patsy and Frank, who own and manage the academy) not to push her. They are going to let her pace herself until she gains more confidence. She did very well, though. Cut her hands on the reins pretty badly, but survived. She has developed a great riding posture. Handles posting quite well and has begun to trot. I'm pleased.

We scared hell out of Mary when we got home. I ran in the house and said we needed a doctor. Mary came out and turned white when she saw Kate's bloody hands. Then we howled. Mary was furious, but we thought it was great.

We spent the day cleaning the house, washing glasses, etc., and then went to the 7:30 p.m. Mass at Ahane. All the old wind-blown bachelors were in the back of church. They reminded me of the people I knew as a kid who used to come in from the country for Mass at St. James. Dead ringers. Wizened faces, calloused hands, and spanking clean, but threadbare clothes.

We spent the rest of the evening preparing for tomorrow's onslaught.

Sunday, November 25. Having left about ninety percent of our utensils, china, silver, and crystal at home, we were extremely fortunate to have the support of Martha Laffan, Dierdre O'Sullivan, and Niamh O'Sullivan. With a little cut-and-paste, Mary was able to put together a stunning banquet table.

The students started to arrive in batches. It was a beautiful, crisp fall day, and they all walked out from school. As I saw the early arrivals coming down the road, the first thing that crossed my mind was— no beer! They hadn't brought the one thing I'd asked them to pick up. We had wine and a little beer, but not enough for twelve college students. Two other groups arrived and brought an additional four bottles of wine, so we put them in for a quick chill and everyone was happy. It wasn't that kind of a party anyway. They were here to eat!! And they did.

It was a tremendous afternoon, everyone sharing memories of past Thanksgivings with their families. Mary had done it up right. She had a huge turkey, mashed potatoes and gravy, creamed onions, cranberries, squash, a variety of vegetables, ambrosia salad—the works. Two of the kids mashed the potatoes, another basted the turkey, and someone else poured the wine. It was just like a family affair and they loved every minute of it. A couple of the kids even puddled up a bit during dinner—thinking of home, obviously. Several mentioned that it was their first Thanksgiving away and how grateful they were to be sharing it with us.

About 7:00, the first shift decided to leave. I didn't want them walking on the Dublin Road. It's unlit at night and dangerous for pedestrians, so I offered to take them back to school in small groups: four the first trip, five the second, and four the third. (Actually, thirteen had shown up.) I had to stop for gas but had no cash with me so I charged ten Pounds on a credit card. It was only the second time I'd used one since we came over, and I hated to do it. Not only are the banks charging over nineteen percent interest, the dollar has sunk like a rock on the international exchange. The Irish pound now costs over one dollar and eighty cents.

The last group wanted me to stop at the Stables with them. We got there and nobody had any cash. Two of them disappeared and came back in a couple of minutes. They had gone to the ATM at the Bank of Ireland. One said he had six pounds left after cashing out; the other said he had six pounds left when he punched in. Nothing has changed since I was in school.

Monday, November 26. Mary dropped me off at school. I had lots of odds and ends. David Brown, one of yesterday's participants, showed up in the office and wanted to chat.

He's an exceptional young man. A twenty-one-year-old Boston University student (like all the rest, he's here on an exchange program), Dave tutors in the slums. He has a great social conscience and he's both bright and mature. He came by just for some general avuncular advice.

Tuesday, November 27. Kate was sick this morning. I called school and asked them to prepare her books and homework. Mary would pick them up after a morning walk with Pat Ellis and Margaret Stapleton. I stayed home and wrote.

Later in the day, John Stapleton stopped in the office and I filled him in on what I'd been doing on an American Studies program. He wants to meet Thursday to set up a lecture schedule for the next term.

Kate was a little perkier when I got home. We had dinner and then sat around the fire talking.

Wednesday, November 28. We woke up to a heavy frost, a pea soup fog, and freezing cold. The puddles in the street were frozen over—almost unheard of at this time of year. The radio said the driving was hazardous.

I walked Kate up to the Dublin Road. We were at the end of our road when she noticed John Foley, a fourteen-year-old who lives up the road from us. She immediately suggested that I might want to go home at that point. I left and she slowed her pace noticeably, no doubt to allow John to catch up. I'm adjusting, but...

From my office, the fog was so thick I couldn't even see the Shannon. It was eerie.

Thursday, November 29. This was not a big day on the accomplishments chart, but I did manage to spend an hour and a half with John Stapleton on the schedule and assignments for the next two terms. It looks as though I will be doing the Graduate seminars for David Coombes, International Relations for Nick Rees, and perhaps a few faculty-oriented lectures. In addition, John has suggested that I take over some of the co-op student visitations. This means traveling around Ireland to see how the students are doing in their off-campus work experiences. I leaped at the opportunity. Hopefully, Mary and Kate could join me on a few trips.

There was a faculty gathering tonight in the White House pub on O'Connell Street. Mary copped out on me at the last minute, but insisted that I go. It was a great evening with many outside guests (including, I think, the Finnish Ambassador). The crowd moved on to a disco at closing time and we ended up jitterbugging and philosophizing until 3:00 a.m.

Mary was up when I got home and we talked for another hour. She demanded that I insist that she goes next time.

Friday, November 30. I had a meeting with some folks from the Business College today. They are interested in my teaching courses on U.S. Trade policy, and the relationship of the business community to the U.S. Government.

Saturday, December 1. Today was very quiet. Mary took Kate horseback riding. I loafed and read. In the afternoon, the three of us went on a walking tour of the waterfront—the new quays, a Civic Center, the under-restoration ruins of King John's Castle, the Church of Ireland Cathedral of St. Mary. The Cathedral was founded in 1168. It was taken over during the Cromwellian period and after the Treaty of Limerick (1691) ended up in Protestant hands permanently. It has been the Anglican Cathedral ever since. It is classic twelfth century Gothic architecture. The interior is done in cut stone, oak beams, and burnished mahogany Gothic woodwork. Incredible craftsmanship.

We went home for dinner and afterward scooped up all the little kids in the neighborhood and took them for a long walk. On our way home, Niamh O'Sullivan came out and invited everyone in for tea.

This was at 10:30! I begged off, but Mary and Kate went. They didn't get home until 2:30. They had sat gabbing by the fire. As they say here, when God made time, He made lots of it.

Sunday, December 2. This morning was obviously laid-back, especially for the ladies of the house. I biked in to Ryan's and picked up the *Sunday Tribune* and the *Sunday (London) Times.*

We went to the Jesuit Church at 5:15.

After dinner, the girls were content to sit and read. I went out for a walk about 10:00 on the Dublin Road. It's unlit, but I was careful. Finnegan's pub was packed so I stopped in to see what was happening.

I was amazed at the people I knew. It was a very colorful evening—old men in caps drinking their pints of Guinness, an eighty-year-old singing in Irish. A neighbor whom I only know by sight came over and introduced himself. Paeder O'Sullivan—yes, another one! We had a nice chat. It is very strange for Irishmen to go out of their way to say hello. They tend to be rather shy, contrary to the popular notions about Irish gregariousness. The place closed at 11:00, so we left and he walked with me as far as our driveway. We stopped in front of the house and another neighbor came by on his way home from the Black Swan. Patrick O'Sullivan, my next-door neighbor, heard us and came out. We all stood there and talked for an hour. What a place!

Monday, December 3. I watched Mary Robinson's inauguration on television at school. It was an impressive ceremony for a small country. The final irony (for a liberal woman elected in a conservative male-dominated country) came when she received a salute from the Defense Forces. Brian Lenihan had been Minister for Defense as well as deputy Leader when he was sacked.

My first exam was from 4:00 to 6:00. I stayed around to see if there would be any anguished cries. None came. Mary picked me up for dinner and about 9:00 we went next door to the O'Sullivans' to watch a tape of the inaugural.

I read for a while and then went for a walk up to Finnegan's where I was accosted by what I thought was an old sot. He told me he had seen me on the way to Mass in Ahane a few times and that I looked like someone who had emigrated to England forty years ago. (I wonder how old I look now!) Someone named Enright. I said no. When it became clear that I was a Yankee, he launched off in to the Kennedys. He was sitting at this very bar when they broke in with the news from Dallas, according to him. Of course, that would have been at 8:30 a.m. Irish time and the pubs don't open 'til midday here, but the story was too good and I wasn't going to interrupt.

He had also seen Ted Kennedy in Limerick and had virtually memorized Teddy's remarks: "When I get back to Washington, I'm going into the White House and tell the President about the warm welcome I've received in Limerick..."

The old man, who finally told me his name was Tommy Berkery, said that as Kennedy left, he went into the Franciscan church to say the Rosary and to pray that Teddy would never be killed in a plane crash—Kennedy was on his way to Shannon at the time—and that when he read in the papers sometime afterward how a plane in which Kennedy was riding had crashed in Massachusetts and several people had died but Kennedy had not—then he knew his prayers had been answered. It was a marvelous case of Irish fantasy wrapped around a piece of reconstructive mental surgery.

I don't think I was there for more than forty-five minutes, but when this fellow got through with me, he had talked about so many issues, I felt I had been there for a week. He even managed to get in a word about how he knew Brian Lenihan.

"How?" I asked.

He had seen him at a wake in Limerick and they had nodded to each other and he knew Brian was his friend. Where the hell was Barry Fitzgerald when I needed him!

Tuesday, December 4. I picked up the exam papers today and began correcting. So many kids seemed to miss the point of the questions that I put the papers away for awhile.

I had lunch with Prof. Coombes regarding the Masters program. It was very enlightening. He's a bit of an eccentric, very British (Oxford), suitably arrogant, but witty and fun to be with. He is fascinated by America and would like to teach there at some point.

After lunch, I worked on a few more exam papers and then went to the Library to print out a bibliography for the American Studies modules. I really needed to get into the Library of Congress computer base to find out what was available in the States.

Wednesday, December 5. I spent a good part of the day correcting exam papers and then walked over to the Stables for a cup of coffee with Fr. Gerry Myers, the chaplain. He invited me to come over to the Salesian retreat on the Clare Coast (Spanish Point) and spend a quiet weekend. He noted, however, that it would cost a couple bottles of "exceptionally good stuff." I might have been shocked if it weren't for my Jesuit training.

Thursday, December 6. John Stapleton came by the office and told me to be sure to attend the Plassey Technology Center's Christmas party. The Center is a business executives' group affiliated with the University. He said in all likelihood, they would love to have me lecture at their seminars—for a fee. I liked that "for a fee" part, especially since everything I am doing here is on the cuff.

I finished the European Integration papers. What a chore. I had to give two D+s. The papers were awful. It killed me, but if the external examiner happened to look at those papers and I had given a higher grade, my own credibility would have been questioned.

I worked on the Politics exams all afternoon.

There was a little tension building up at home this week. I think it's a precursor to the Christmas Blues.

Friday, December 7. Pearl Harbor Day—almost fifty years on.

It snowed in the mountains overnight. I could look up at Keeper Hill (the highest point in the area) and the Clare Hills and see the white peaks. It was a beautiful morning, though. Sunny and crisp.

I finished the Politics exams papers this afternoon. What a relief! There were some very funny extracts in the essays, though: "If lobbyists or pressure groups are caught bribing a representative or official, they are libel (sic) to be discredited." "Ideas for legislation come from think tanks who have rational ideas." "There are three major parts of the American political system... the Supreme Court is seen as the minor part in the Trilogy." "In the words of Aristotle, "pressure groups" form the architect of our society."

Mary came in for a Women's Studies Program, which ran most of the afternoon. It broke up around 6:00 and we walked over to the Stables. She had been asked to join the ladies at the Hurler's Pub not too far from the campus. I insisted—said it would do her good. After we made arrangements for Kate to spend the evening with the O'Sullivans, who are nighthawks, I dropped Mary off. The ladies politely informed me that I was not invited to stay, so I went home, had dinner alone, and then decided to go in to the Black Swan to see if any of the neighbors were around. I met Pat Foley who lives down the road. His son John is Kate's pal. Pat's daughter just got out of Kuwait by the skin of her teeth before the Iraqis overran the country. She rode across the desert in a jeep with nine other escapees.

We sat and talked for a while and then the crowd gathered around for a card tournament—something called "45." I was invited to stay, but since I didn't know the game and they obviously took it seriously, I was a fish out of water, and bowed out gracefully.

Saturday, December 8. I took Kate riding this morning. The snow on the mountains was beautiful, but the weather was fierce. I damn near froze watching her trot and canter. She was good. Very confident and moving along at a nice comfortable pace. She rode "Wallace" today, a gentle roan who must be thirty-years-old, but who still performs well.

After dinner, everyone was content to sit in front of the fire and read. All of a sudden, it dawned on us. This was a Holy Day and we had forgotten to go to church. I think that was a first for us.

Sunday, December 9. Mary wanted to go to the Monaleen church to hear the choir. Someone told her it was a lovely Mass. We sat there in a freezing cold, blustery stone building, with no choir, no chemistry, and very little interest, while a genuine Druid harangued us from the pulpit. It was awful. I should have learned my lesson after the children's Mass at the Salesian church. I don't know where Mary finds some of these people.

We had Martha Laffan and her four kids over for our Advent wreath gathering.(Each night during Advent, we have traditionally gathered around the symbolic wreath with the appropriate readings and carols in preparation for Christmas. We started when Kate was just a baby.) It was really enjoyable and very "family."

To give the evening the proper Irish dimension, we finished up with tea and biscuits—and talk.

Monday, December 10. Had a funny experience today. Mary and I were about to get into the car to go to school when Noreen Connell walked by. (Her husband Jerry had brought us the load of fuel a few weeks ago.) She said Jerry had tried to get out to open the manual railroad gates for the early morning Dublin train, but couldn't get the car door unfrozen, so he had to walk the length of the tracks up to the Murroe Road to close the gates. Talk about primitive conditions! We have a set of manual gates on our street as well, about two hundred yards away, operated by a family named Bridgeman. The trains are no disturbance. They hardly make any noise and are past in under sixty seconds a few times a day.

Tuesday, December 11. I felt as though I had a "bug" when I woke up, but I walked Kate up to the bus and then went in to the university.

I had a lot of work to do on my modules project and so I went in to the Library to spend some time with Patti Punch on the computer. We tapped into the Library of Congress in Washington via the BLAZE (British Library) network in London. It's mind boggling for someone like me whose mechanical expertise doesn't extend beyond a fingernail file.

I recovered as the day progressed, and ate like a hog at dinner. Even had some homemade apple pie alamode, no less. Got a big fire going, and we did the Advent wreath.

Wednesday, December 12. Went in to school early this morning trying to catch the first mail pickup. I had all the Christmas cards to deposit and figured it would probably take two to three weeks to get to the States. It was pretty quiet around the place.

Eoin O'Sullivan came by the office with more exam papers, so I really didn't get out of that chore as soon as I'd expected.

Thursday, December 13. Yet more exam papers surfaced today, so I was faced with more essays.

We had a little tiff at home—no screaming or door banging—just a quiet departure. I think the financial picture is getting to me. The dollar is pitiful on the international exchange. I haven't unloaded our other car at home, the housing market in Washington is in a state of collapse and, as of right now, I haven't programmed a regular stable income. Anyway, I went out and walked my frustrations off.

Friday, December 14. Activity was rather sparse at school, although I did notice a number of scientific and mathematics faculty running around with computer printouts, talking to themselves. I can't figure out what those people do.

Mary came in and met me when I had finished going over the marked papers with Eoin and Nick. My grading was about on target.

We stopped at the Stables for a few minutes. Big crowd—but almost no students. Very civilized without the jukebox.

It was an early night after dinner and the Advent readings.

Saturday, December 15. Mary took Kate riding this morning. It was her turn

I puttered around the house and checked out our oil fuel consumption. It appears that we used about five hundred liters since October 1, approximately one third of the tank. At that rate, we should make it through the winter all right.

Kate went off to play after riding, and Mary and I went in to the city. There were dozens of choral groups floating around town and the city looked very Christmas-y. We stopped at one bandbox, bought a carol book from a St. Vincent de Paul volunteer. (The group was singing a lot of Irish carols, and we didn't know the lyrics.) We sang with the audience in the street. It was fun.

Slow night. Dinner, Advent, reading. I'm rereading "Uncle Vanya" and some other humorous classics.

Sunday, December 16. I was up early this morning. It's been damp and coolish in the morning all week, but the weather has been unseasonably dry. Some days have been spectacular.

I walked in to Ryan's and picked up the Tribune and the Times. We went to the 11:00 at Ahane. It was a great Mass with music and a good sermon—there is no consistency in this place at all. I've thought to myself a hundred times that the people and the events are like the country roads. One never knows what's just around the corner.

Kate went off with her gang. It was her first real free weekend in several weeks. Mary and I drove over to Ennis to Martin and Betty Ryan's for tea.

After dinner, Niamh O'Sullivan and her three daughters joined us for Advent. It was very enjoyable, if somewhat incomprehensible to the kids.

Monday, December 17. I had meetings with several faculty members today, but each was scratched at the last minute. These are a very unpredictable people. Delightful, but not very reliable. I think they genuinely find appointments and commitments terribly confining.

I started to slip into a bit of a Christmas funk today.

Tuesday, December 18. Didn't really stir out of the house today. I had brought computer printouts of the Library of Congress listings home and began culling out a reference library for American Studies—if it comes to pass. I managed to locate twenty or thirty works, which could form the core of our library.

Still a little "down" today. The prospects don't look particularly encouraging.

This evening I stopped at Finnegan's for about a half hour to catch the local news. Tom Berkery came over. I must look like a "live one." He told me for some wholly unknown reason that he had only been outside County Limerick a couple of times in his life—to Cork, Clare, and Tipperary. He is/was a carpenter. A car-pen' ter, as they say here.

Tommy filled me in on all the week's gossip. He's sixty and looks eighty-five. He's been unemployed for ten years, and only this year, was put on pre-retirement, whatever the hell that is. The dole here is fantastic, but the income taxes to pay for it are outrageous—fifty-four percent on everything over eleven thousand pounds (approximately twenty-thousand dollars at the current rate of exchange). Why there hasn't been a rebellion is beyond me. Perhaps it is because those who aren't on relief know there's a good chance they will be sometime soon, and those who have been are grateful for what they received when they were.

Wednesday, December 19. I had trouble getting myself out of the house and over to school today. It was as though everything were crowding me.

It was sunny but cold and damp. I went for a long bike ride down the Mt. Shannon Road and found a secluded spot on the River where anglers go. It was absolutely serene. The River is calm there, because of its depth, and with the sun, the clouds and the blue sky reflected in the water, it was a magnificent scene.

After dinner, we all went to the Jean Monet Theater at the University for a Limerick Chorale program, complete with readings, traditional Christmas songs from Ireland, Scotland, Wales and England, and a real seanaché who told some marvelous stories. Kate, particularly, got a bang out of it.

We stopped back at Laffan's house afterward. They had gone with us. Kate was so moved by the evening that she actually went to the piano <u>voluntarily</u> and played "Fur Elise" and some other classical pieces. Mirabili dictu.

Thursday, December 20. I went in to the Departmental Christmas Luncheon today. Things seemed a bit better, although it was a bleak and rainy day. Paddy Doran came over to me and apologized for not responding to my enquiries on a number of academic and financial matters. He said he had no idea all the issues I'd been involved with since my arrival, or all the hats I'd been wearing.

Met with Henry Ellis later on. He gave me a much more focused reading on what he would like in American Studies. He wants it at the graduate level although he also sees the need and a place for an undergraduate program as well.

Dr. Bernadette Whelan asked me to lecture her History course in the Summer Term (Easter through June).

All in all, it was a good day at school. My spirits were lifted generally.

Friday, December 21. Mary left me off at school and then went in shopping. There was the usual round of office Christmas parties. The Student Union hosted a gathering for the "working stiffs," to which I was invited as well. It was raucous, with all sorts of local talent. Mary returned and we romped through the rest of the afternoon, singing and dancing.

Kate had done Christmas decorations with one of the girls in the neighborhood all evening and was sound asleep when we got home. The area is so secure; I have no fears about leaving her during the evening, nor does she worry.

Saturday, December 22. I took Kate to Ashroe this morning. She rode "Jerry," who is a younger pony and more stubborn than either "Wallace" or "Pride." She wasn't happy because she had to work. Wallace is old and docile, and Pride is smart and responsive, but Jerry is Jerry, and he has to be goaded.

The kids are trotting and jumping now and working on their posture.

We stopped near the ring (fairy) fort on the way home—we now have learned where it is—and cut down piles of cedar branches, holly, rhododendron leaves and some foliage we couldn't identify. It is great for Christmas decorations.

We all went to bed early, as tomorrow promised to be a long day. True to a tradition we had started years ago in Virginia, we are hosting a large Christmas party for the entire neighborhood.

Sunday, December 23. After I went in and picked up the newspapers, we spent the day vacuuming, polishing, building fires in the living room and the den, and setting things out.

We had no idea how our party would be received or whether indeed anyone would even come. By and large, people in Ireland simply don't throw big open houses at their homes.

The postman arrived—on a Sunday yet—and delivered about a dozen pieces of mail. A very pleasant surprise.

We all showered in mid-afternoon and then went in to the 5:15 at Sacred Heart, the Jesuit Church. We have met the Sunday celebrant, Fr. Paddy Tyrell, and he is a peach. He gave a great sermon on the Nativity today.

At seven o'clock we walked up to Laffans' at the end of the road to begin a neighborhood choral gathering we had planned earlier. We all had candles or flashlights (the Irish call them torches) and sheet music. We started with a Jamaican family who lived across the street from the Laffans. He is with some corporation headquartered at Shannon Development. They couldn't join us because of a prior commitment, but they were obviously appreciative that we stopped. The next stop was warmly received and we picked up another caroler.

Mary and Kate had baked up a storm—gingerbread cookies, brownies, eggnog, sandwiches.

After the walking serenade, which was a smashing success, the crowd hit our house and came in. They were joined by all sorts of additional neighbors, mostly the husbands who hadn't sung. (I was the solo husband in the group.) They were all enthusiastic about the notion of the party and even more so about the prospect of meeting their neighbors—not us—the people they'd lived next door to for years and never met! It was interesting introducing couples to their own neighbors. All in all, I guess we had somewhere around sixty or seventy people in the house. It was a great family gathering. The adults sat in clusters, a few around the open fires. Kids ran everywhere. One young guy from up the street dressed up as Santa Claus unknown to us, and showed up at the door to the delight of everyone.

Monday, December 24. The Laffans invited us for dinner after which we planned to go to Midnight Mass at Glenstal, the Benedictine Abbey in Murroe.

The Mass was very poignant. I felt as though it was the first real Mass I'd been to in twenty-five years. The Office started about 11:30—in Latin. The Gregorian Chant still conjures up great memories for me. There was an abundance of incense and the combination of the sounds and the scents was exhilarating.

The Abbey itself, though only about sixty-five years old, is constructed like a mediaeval fortress-church. It is made of hewn stone, with vaulted ceilings and ceiling frescoes, hard kneeling benches and straightback pews. Although there were heaters about three quarters of the way up the walls, the place was extremely cold. I could see my breath, and even with warm clothes and galoshes, I was still uncomfortable—at least physically. The kids thoroughly enjoyed the program. It was a novelty, among other things. It was certainly a "first" for Kate.

When the Mass was over, everyone was invited back to the adjoining school (a Benedictine prep) for tea, sandwiches and Christmas cake, which is like a fruit cake, only more so. It has marzipan, and frosting, and loads of whisky.

It was pouring outside and the wind was howling. As a matter of fact, the rain and blowing had lent a special aura of mystery to the Mass, the monks in their cowls and robes, and the candles flickering all over the church. I guess all we needed was thunder and lightning.

The drive back was nerve-wracking. Martha forgot we were following her and drove like hell. The rain was coming in sheets and I tried to keep up with her taillights as we whipped around hairpin curves. I had visions of us being found in a glen sometime in March.

Tuesday, December 25. No one surfaced very early on Christmas morning. We ate in pieces and when Kate came down we had Santa. It was very pleasant with a roaring fire in the den. We had a lot of laughs and I don't think there was a tear shed over our absence from home. We were all too busy, and having too much fun.

Kate, of course, couldn't wait to share her loot with her friends and so she was soon off around the neighborhood.

We went next door to O'Sullivan's for a drop-in, and then out to Noel and Caroline Mulcahy's in Castleconnell. It was Noel's sixtieth birthday. He is a Professor and Dean of the College of Science and Engineering.

Several relatives in the States called with holiday greetings, but we couldn't get through to anyone there.

Wednesday, December 26. This is known as St. Stephen's Day in Ireland. It is a national holiday. I've asked all around and no one can give a definitive reason why.

I think it's just a practical day off after Christmas, given a Christian veneer. It's also called Wren (ran) Day on which singers and mimes traditionally go through towns and countryside performing and collecting money either for themselves or for charity. We had some Wren singers stop at the house. I took a picture of them with their faces all painted and their clothes bedecked with baubles. I gave them thirty pence for their efforts.

31

There probably would have been more participants during the day, but the wind and the rain were brutal. The radio said the winds have been gale force off the coast. I don't think I've ever lived through such rain and blowing. The front door actually blew open. The chain was on it so it only V-ed inward. I suppose it could have come off the hinges.

We drove over to David and Eva Coombes in Castleconnell for what we thought was a reception. Instead we found a small handful of very colorful personalities gathered casually around a refectory table: David and Eva, who teach French at the Abbey School, Fr. Brian Murphy, a noted author and historian who also teaches there, Lloyd Melnik, the graduate student from Scarsdale, and Kathy Herbert, a prominent newscaster on RTE, the national radio network. Her father is a noted publican, a former member of the European Parliament, and a retired Fianna Fail Party activist.

The conversation was quick, witty, at times fiery, always literate. We ranged all over the globe, and didn't leave until 7:30.

Thursday, December 27. This was a very pleasant morning. The St. Stephen's Day races here in Limerick were rescheduled for today. The track was underwater yesterday.

I went in to Ryan's to buy a paper and pick up some odds and ends. The stores are all closed. This is the third day in a row. Where else would banks, government services, stores, etc. all stay closed for three days? The newspapers don't even try to publish.

What's the point? No one would come to work to get the paper out, and no one, save a few crazy Yankees, would buy it anyway. Since Christmas fell on a Tuesday this year, most places simply closed down from last Saturday until tomorrow. If one is prepared, it's not a bad idea.

In the evening, we stopped over at Pat and Judy Foley's, down the road from us. We had a very pleasant visit but were a little shocked to learn that in the ten years they've lived there, we were the first neighbors to set foot in their house. For all their affability, the Irish are generally still a shy people.

House-calling doesn't come easily to them.

Friday, December 28. We started out with a full agenda of things to do, but as in most Irish adventures, the chores got sidetracked. Mary barely got out of her bathrobe all day. She wanted to bake some brownies and take them to Pat and Henry Ellis. Of course, I had forgotten to get the walnuts and baking powder, but rather than go all the way back to the shopping center and fight the crowds, I drove from shop to shop looking for the items. Considering that petrol is five dollars a gallon, I figure the brownies cost about a pound each.

Saturday, December 29. Fr. Paddy Tyrell came out and celebrated Mass for the three of us in the den. It was a wonderful Anniversary gift—very personal and very moving. We capped it off with tea and biscuits in the kitchen afterwards.

I drove Kate and a few friends up to O'Reilly's (the video shop) for an hour or so. They were supposed to be picked up by Madeline Bridgeman (the railroad gatekeeper) who never showed. There was no phone at the shop so the girls walked back on the railroad tracks in the dark. It was scary, Kate told me, but too late to do anything.

Kate set the table for an Anniversary dinner, complete with linen and candles. We had pizza! And laughs. Mom and Mary's parents all called. This is a very poignant day for us all. Seventeen years ago, we began what became a traditional luncheon each year. The group included my folks, Mary's, Jack and Millie Mc Auliffe, and Fr. Jack Morse. Now, Fr. Jack and my Pop are dead, the McAuliffes and my mother are in Syracuse, Mary's parents live in Florida and she and I are in Ireland.

It started snowing in earnest just before dinner. Very pretty, but the roads were a mess. The lads in the neighborhood were out for a good snowball fight. Fun to watch the novelty of it, since there's not much snow that falls in this area except on the mountaintops.

I built a great fire and the girls both settled down to read. With the snow falling right outside the window, it looked like one of those Bing Crosby movies from the forties.

Sunday, December 30. I rode in to Annacotty for the papers and almost fell off my bicycle twice. The road was a sheet of ice.

Roused the family and we went to the 11:00 at Ahane. Again, the back row was full of old and middle-aged bachelors who looked like they stepped out of a photo album from the farm in Pompey, New York.

It was a fairly uneventful day.

Monday, December 31. Peter Rolls, our young banker next door, who finally got his family moved in by Christmas, stopped by to invite me over to Castletroy Golf Club later. He said he thought he'd go about 3:00. Would I be interested in a game of snooker? Said he'd call before he was ready to leave. I said yes.

During the day, I lost track of the time and he showed up at the door at 2:55. I asked if he could give me ten minutes to shave and he replied that he had to meet a guy promptly at 3:00. This was the first time I'd ever met anyone in Ireland who was actually on time and who couldn't wait ten minutes. I thought to myself: either he's going to the very top of his profession, or he'll be burned out before he's thirty-five, or he was adopted at birth and really isn't even Irish.

We were invited to Jim and Niamh O'Sullivan's across the road for a New Year's Eve gathering. Maybe we've started something in the neighborhood. We had planned to go in to some festivities at Arthur's Quay on the River, but it was cold, raining, and blustery. Besides, several people said the place would be crawling with drunks and punks. We didn't need that, so we opted out. Thought instead we'd go in for the official opening of the new Waterfront and the Treaty 300 ceremonies. This is the three-hundredth Anniversary of the Treaty of Limerick, which officially forced the Wild Geese to flee Ireland in the seventeenth century.

O'Sullivan's was a field day. They had about ten couples sitting along the walls around a big open fire—all laughing and talking. It looked like the back room at an Irish-American funeral parlor.

Tuesday, January 1. We didn't get up until almost 2:00 in the afternoon. I had coffee and scones and walked over to Jim and Niamh's to say thanks for the party. Jim was at Dierdre and Pat's returning chairs—the ones we'd borrowed for Thanksgiving dinner. Niamh and I walked to the other O'Sullivans, and Dierdre asked us in for a cup of tea. I called Mary and she came over. There we were again, sitting, talking, laughing. Pat was/is quite an athlete. Played lots of Gaelic League matches and was a Cup winner in badminton, which is incredibly popular here. It was fascinating listening to him tell how they trained for badminton. I had thought of the game as sort of a backyard lark.

We inquired about an evening Mass at Ahane and everyone said there were no Masses anywhere on New Year's Day. What about the Holy Day? They said the Church decided a few years ago to shift the Holy Day to January 6. It was pointless to open a church on January 1 for an assembly constituted mostly by hangovers, snoozes, snorts, and farts. Made sense to me.

Mary had picked up some spare ribs yesterday. Ever since I was a kid, we always had spare ribs on New Year's Day. I think it was a custom Mom and Pop inherited from the farm—the pork, which had been slaughtered in the fall, was well-smoked or salted by January.

Mary parboiled the ribs this afternoon and then popped them into the oven when we came home. Brussels sprouts, crisp spare ribs, fried potatoes, and homemade applesauce (from Noel and Caroline Mulcahy's orchard)—a great American tradition. Kate said grace and thanked God that in seven months we'd be home!

Wednesday, January 2. Today was one of those on-again-off-again weather days. It was balmy in the morning and the sun was out, but by the time I had had breakfast, showered and dressed, it had rained three times and dropped ten degrees.

I drove in to school. It was like a morgue, although some of the support staff were on hand. The mail arrived and it was a pile. I went through most of it, then turned to my paperwork—I had to flesh out those modules.

When I got home, we had a repeat performance with the mail. There was a ton of it.

About ten o'clock in the evening, Kate and I decided to go for a night walk. The moon was bright and the clouds were moving at a tremendous clip. The ground wind was cold, but the road was relatively dry, so off we went. It was pleasantly nippy (we were dressed warmly), and the weather changed, as did the sky patterns, about a half dozen times before we got home. It's one of the wonders of living on an island so near the sea-blown west winds.

As we walked along, Kate reminded me of a deciduous tree at the end of our road that was barren in November.

The gnarled branches had reached up like witches' arms against a harvest moon. There had been two birds perched high on the branches—like something out of a Disney ghost story.

She described it in detail. Obviously, one of the salient memories of Ireland indelibly imprinted in her mind. I'm pleased.

It was a great father-daughter evening.

Thursday, January 3. We had planned to go to Lissycasey today to visit the Hehirs. The early morning radio indicated the roads were icy all over the country, but particularly around Limerick and in the West. It was cold as hell, and it was raining/sleeting. We decided to write and do odd jobs around the house.

Mary told me an interesting story. She said that Pat Foley had approached her at the O'Sullivan party and told her how appreciative they were about having these two 'very educated' people in, and how they feared they might be embarrassed. He said they were quite relieved after they met us and they really enjoyed our visit. It's amazing how we sometimes perceive others as occupants of different planets.

Mary and Kate cleaned the house, and Kate went in to Ryan's for some sandwich bread. Incredible! We must have had several tons of food in the house a few days ago, and today we didn't even have a loaf of bread in the freezer.

I went for a long walk in the evening and stopped at Finnegan's. It was very quiet. I think most people are broke at this point. I ran into a painting contractor I had met there previously, Liam O'Shea, and we fell to talking about the income tax system in Ireland. I asked him how people survive with taxes at the fifty percent + level, and he said simply, —

"They cheat. No one could survive otherwise."

He told me a story about a cash job he was doing and how the revenue boys watched the house for four days. They obviously knew he was going to take the money and run, so one day they closed in. He made believe he was the owner who had to go out to the barn to feed the chickens or cows or whatever and he just kept on going through the fields. Left his paint and brushes, ladders, etc. and had to collect them under cover of night. Funny story—probably played out a hundred times a day all over Ireland.

Friday, January 4. I reflected this morning on a conversation I had the other night with two guys who work at Shannon Airport. They were refueling U.S. aircraft destined for the Middle East. The planes, according to them, contained body bags. As horrible as it is, it's about the only immediacy the conflict out there has here. God, this place can be isolated. Even the radio music is straight out of the late Fifties and early Sixties. It's like a time warp. Conversations with home, however, point to a war within the next two weeks, and that brings reality a little closer.

It was cold, damp, and overcast this morning. Our firewood is all used up, and we've only one packet of turf briquettes. Still have a bag of cut turf and lots of coal, though. Folks tell us it is inordinately cold and damp now. Should dry up in January.

After dinner, one of my graduate students, Lloyd Melnik, called. Asked if we could go out and talk. I picked him up at school and we stopped at the Black Swan, just to give him some of the country flavor.

While we were standing there talking, I saw a fellow who looked very familiar, but I couldn't figure out why. I looked at him two or three times and he glanced back nervously, wondering, I'm sure, who the hell I was and why I was staring at him. It finally hit me.

I walked over and said, "Didn't I see you on the altar at Glenstal Abbey?"

"Yes," he said, "I'm Brother Gregory."

What a country! I've met two Benedictine monks since I've been here—one at a well-oiled party and the other in a pub!

They're predicting gale winds tomorrow—up to one hundred miles an hour.

Saturday, January 5. Mary turned forty-seven today. Actually Kate and I had wished her a Happy Birthday at 12:15 last night. She said she wanted her coffee in bed and then peace and quiet. Kate and I had breakfast and then left for Ashroe.

Kate has improved steadily. She has good posture, strength in the saddle, and great control. I think she's probably ready for serious cantering next week.

Shortly after we arrived, the wind and the rain came. We were in the riding arena, which has a corrugated tin roof and walls. I thought for sure the building would come down around us. It was frightening, but the show went on as usual.

Mary and I went out for her birthday. (Kate had a friend over for pizza and an overnight.) We went to Chaser O'Brien's in Pallasgreen on the Tipperary Road about fifteen miles from home. On the way, I stopped in Cappamore for gas, and when I opened the door to get out, the door nearly blew off. The wind was so forceful, it sprang the hinges. I had to fight to get the door closed again. I could barely lock it, it was so out-of-kilter.

The electricity went out during dinner, so the whole place was candle-lit. It was very comfortable, though, because there was a fire in every fireplace.

We came out in the pitch dark (everything around us was out as well) and headed home. The car literally rocked and seemed to lose power; such was the ferocity of the head winds. I'd never experienced anything quite like it.

The extent of the damage from the gale winds was hard to determine at that point, but there was a lot of debris in the roads. I actually saw a mattress bouncing end-over-end down the Dublin Road, and the electricity apparently was out all over the country.

Sunday, January 6. The storm was over today, but there was a thick glaze of dirt from the wind and the rain that covered every window in the house.

We all went to the 11:00 at Ahane. The little road was lined with cars for a half-mile in both directions, and the church was packed. I thought it strange, but figured it had something to do with Epiphany. Cars were parked every which way and were being driven the same.

The church was a sardine can. I had noticed a station wagon with a funeral director's name on it parked in front, but assumed it belonged to a parishioner. When I looked around the church, I spotted a casket in front of the altar. It was indeed a funeral Mass—on a Sunday. Mary Ahern (ninety+) had died, and all of Ahane had turned out. Apparently they have this sort of arrangement in Ireland regularly, but a Sunday funeral was a first for me.

About ninety percent of the church went to Communion, and since they have only a center aisle with two lines of communicants heading toward the altar, getting back was like broken-field running, hurtling, and quarterback sneaking all combined. I was bruised, shinned, shoved, elbowed, and stepped on twenty different times going up and back. They can be an incredibly disorganized people. No one would ever think here to direct one line up and the other back.

Every politician in the area was on hand outside the church to pay respects to Mary's family. I felt quite at home "working a funeral."

We decided to go to Lissycasey in the afternoon. It was a lovely day and there was almost no traffic on the road. We made it in about forty-five minutes—a new record—and then proceeded to get lost! We took the wrong turn and ended up on a ridge overlooking the River Fergus, which flows south into the Shannon.

Had a delightful time with the cousins and left before dark so as not to get lost in the bogs.

Monday, January 7. Our power was back on but it was cold both indoors and outside. The snow came furiously for a few minutes, but didn't stick. The radio was full of post-mortems and warnings. Wind and sea damage was in the millions of pounds. Whole beaches, cliffsides, and wharfs from Kilkee to Lahinch were washed away. There was severe damage in Galway, Mayo, Sligo, and Donegal. Terrible flooding in Dublin and West Limerick. Seventeen dead so far. We weren't terribly bad off in our neck of the woods, however, although the winds had been so strong on Saturday that I saw a number of birds attempt aerodynamic lift-offs, lose power, and then plummet to the ground.

The news indicated that roads were bad around here. They're predicting more snow, hail, and heavy winds.

I drove in to the University this morning. Bicycling, more than likely, would have been a fruitless venture.

Someone mentioned that Gerry Myers, the chaplain, had had a heart attack over the holidays —at age thirty-four. The chaplaincy is a terribly stressful job—seventy to eighty hours a week helping students through their crises. The word around school is that he'll be laid up for three months at least.

Tuesday, January 8. The Gulf situation looks pretty bad today. Both sides are saber rattling, and war is apparently imminent.

The local scene was cold and snowy. About zero Celsius, but very damp and uncomfortable. The radio warned of treacherous roads throughout the area. Said the local officials were out "gritting the roads." They don't use sand or salt spreaders as we do in the States. Here, a work crew follows a truck down the road, leveling and then shoveling the periodic piles of dirt and stones that are dropped off the back of the truck. It is a painfully primitive exercise, but it is inexpensive, it is effective, and most of all, it does provide jobs.

It snowed very hard most of the day. Several inches. A rarity in Ireland. They had a foot up in Tipperary. The roads were icy and freezing rain was predicted for overnight.

I had a great snowball fight when I got home. The boys in the neighborhood went after Kate and the other girls. I came to the rescue. My aim was great, and the mastery of scooping up snow and making the snowballs on the run was still intact—but my speed had gone south. The boys nailed me.

I had a threatening letter from the phone company today. Their charges are unitemized and I have refused to pay them without a bill of particulars.

The original bill I received was for one hundred five pounds, and covered two months of equipment rental, plus local calls. The rest of the items were trunk calls (long distance). The problem is that one month's trunk calls were made before we even moved in. The equipment rental and the phone charges overlap, but they do not cover the same period. Without any itemization, customers are left to the tender mercies of the company. It's like taking a cart full of groceries up to the counter and having the clerk say, "That will be fifty pounds" without even looking to see what's in the cart. It's absolutely crazy. The most frustrating part of it is that when I explain my consternation to others, they simply shrug their shoulders and imply, "That's the way it is here." A very Irish reaction.

Wednesday, January 9. It snowed pretty hard again overnight. I didn't trust the double-decker bus Kate normally takes, or the driver for that matter, so I took her to school myself. It was a real 'treat,' challenging drivers who only see snow a few times in their lives.

After an uneventful day at school, I caught the news at 10:00 and went to bed. The radio indicated that the GATT negotiations in Geneva (centering around the problems between the US and the European Community) had fallen apart. Also heard that the Irish Government is printing up gas rationing stamps because of the Middle East situation. Looks pretty grim at this point.

Thursday, January 10. Yesterday's slush turned to ice overnight and the roads were very greasy. I took Kate to school again, without incident. Heard on the news that President Bush had signed an Executive Proclamation, which would give priority to the military for food, gas, etc.

I measured the fuel oil this morning—seven hundred fifty to eight hundred liters—half a tank with three months to go.

Did preparatory work for my International Relations lecture—mostly mental gymnastics. The lecture notes are in good shape, but I want to be sure my responses to the students will be sharp and focused.

Mary and I participated in a lecture/discussion on Church-State relations tonight. Very invigorating.

The group consisted of the two of us, Paddy Lyons, a Benedictine monk (they're everywhere), Tony Davidson, a Presbyterian minister from the North who is now in Limerick, the Church of Ireland chaplain at the University, Michael Nutting, and a handful of social and political activists.

It was a most stimulating evening. In a country that borders on a theocracy, the U.S. experience of separating the churches and the government completely was both intriguing and enlightening.

When we got home, the dog next door was out in back yipping like crazy. I went out to look, and there in the dark was our neighbor Peter Rolls checking his oil tank. He said he thought he'd better fill it up. Might not be able to get any next week.

Friday, January 11. I took Kate in to school and after three scary "near misses" decided the safest place I could be for the day was home. I got out of the car, slid on the icy concrete, and fell against the front door, cracking my head on the brass knob. I thought I had a concussion but it was just a severe jolt.

Saturday, January 12. Kate cantered and jumped at Ashroe this morning. She was on "Wallace," and she was full of herself when it was over. Had to share the experience with every kid in the neighborhood.

Since the house was crammed with cackling, giggling girls, Mary and I decided to go for a drive and left in the direction of Adare. It is an absolutely beautiful little village about a half hour from Limerick on the road to Tralee and Killarney. It is an exceptionally quiet and clean area (last year it won the 'Tidy Towns' award—I think the title is a hoot). At the suggestion of the owner of the Mustard Seed Restaurant, we walked over to Adare Manor, a splendid old estate that has been converted into a gracious inn/restaurant/conference center with a tournament golf course. Mary corrected me on the architectural style. The crenelated walls and towers looked Norman to me, but the building is officially Tudor Gothic. The grounds are magnificent and huge.

We must have walked two miles—a good part of the time along the banks of the River Maige. We looked directly across at the old Norman Castle ruins (home of the Earls of Desmond-the Fitzgeralds) and the Franciscan Friary. Both dated from the fourteenth to fifteenth centuries. We walked across the "wishing bridge," built in the 13th century and still in use. We were lost in time.

A few minutes later we heard on the car radio that the U.S. House and Senate had voted to go to war.

Sunday, January 13. It was a bright dry day, but even with the sun, it was bitter cold. I made my ritual trip in to Ryan's for the papers.

They were full of war stories—real graphic items about poison gases, body counts, past terrorism, prospective terrorism, rapes, torture, etc. It was frightening. Page after page of it.

Kate has asked me at least a half dozen times in the last week, "Pop, are we going to have World War III?" I explained how difficult it is to contain wars but I didn't think it would be a global conflict.

"We're safe," I assured her, "and they won't hit Ireland or your grandparents."

"But," she followed up, "what about Washington?" (where she had grown up and where most of her friends lived).

I could only mumble something about our superb defense network.

Monday, January 14. There was a pall hanging over the University today. The conflict seems inevitable and everyone feels so helpless. One can't help but think of Europe blundering into World War I.

Nick Rees came by the office. He had just concluded the first segment of the International Relations lectures. I'll be meeting the students shortly and he wanted to fill me in on the class and the atmosphere. There are only 23 in the group, so the course will be both intense and personal.

Tuesday, January 15. We finished off all the Christmas card addresses. We'll send letters and pictures out this week. We had about one hundred cards – many from people who haven't corresponded in years but who felt an urge to write to us in Ireland, and some from people we didn't even know, but who had read about our venture in the newspaper at home. The cards were a great boost for us all, although we actually didn't have a serious "Christmas blues" problem.

At lunch today, all conversation centered on the war. The perception of the U.S. had been skewed by events. Irish "green card" holders in the States were at risk if there was a general conscription at home, and Shannon Airport would be at risk here if the terror goes amuck because Shannon is the refueling point for U.S. aircraft.

I dropped into Finnegan's after dinner to see what the local folks were saying. No anti-Yank sentiment. Just resignation. According to news reports, the war is five hours away.

Wednesday, January 16. The war didn't start last night, but there was a creepy air of anticipation today. I still think it will happen and with a ferocity!

It was quiet at school. I took some gentle ribbing but nothing serious. I suspect if things go wrong out there I could be in for a little hassle from my colleagues.

I stopped over at the Stables on the way home. It was almost 6:00—news time—and the place was packed, but the TV wasn't even turned on! I talked with lots of people, and the Gulf only came up once. It was as though no one wanted to discuss the inevitable—sheer avoidance behavior. Boy, are the Irish good at that!

Kate said at dinner that some kids had started needling her at school about the "American war."

There is a debate going on in the press here about whether or not the Government can let the U.S. refuel at Shannon without the Parliament's approval. One side represents a long-standing Irish neutrality sentiment, the other, a feeling of if-we're-going-to-be-in-the-EC-let's-drop-this-neutrality-nonsense.

Still no war news at 10:00.

Thursday, January 17. I got up about 5:45 and turned on the BBC. They said war had broken out six hours ago, that over one hundred installations had been destroyed already. I'd like to think it could be over in days, but I fear a "street war" in the desert.

I was frankly rather nervous about Kate going to school today. My concern was not over her schoolmates and the potential taunts. It was much more basic and frightening for me—kidnapping! I know that the IRA provisionals are in the area and I know of their relationship with the Arab (particularly Libyan) extremists. Kate resisted and I relented. I walked her up to the Dublin Road and we had a fun talk. When we got close to the intersection and in view of the boys who ride the bus with her, she turned and said, "Pop, you'd better get home. You know Mom is all alone." I howled. She had burst my bubble. She's fantastic.

Mary had a meeting in town and dropped me off at the University. I was apprehensive about some of the academic community, but talked with many of them and felt no hostility.

There was a rumor around that a bomb went off in London—but no confirmation. Apparently a few allied planes had been hit.

I walked over to the Stables about at 5:30. A news special was on. I was surprised that the lads were standing around by the dozens in front of the screen watching the conflict footage. Interesting sociology. They didn't seem to be interested yesterday. Today, the ballgame was actually being played and they were mesmerized. Even the jukebox was silent.

38

After a quick dinner, a recap of the day, and plenty of bantering with Kate, Mary and I went back to school for the Church/State series. The speaker was a very articulate woman lecturer at the Church of Ireland Seminary. She was a biblical scholar and a good teacher. She set up a matrix for the Jewish relationship to political governance—thus foreshadowing the conflict between Christ and the Romans. It was well researched and well executed.

We stopped at Finnegan's on the way home and chatted briefly with Willie Quirke, a cattle farmer from the neighborhood. We all laughed over the fact that the RTE (national network) hadn't even carried the war story except as another piece of the day's news. The Parliament even delayed debate on Ireland's involvement (allowing the U.S. to refuel at Shannon legally) until tomorrow, by which time the issue will be moot. Oh, for the life of a third rate power!

At midnight the bombing, temporarily halted during the day, had been reinstituted with a fury.

Friday, January 18. I turned on the radio at 6:20 to learn that Israel had been attacked. The news was sketchy. I prayed because I feared the whole situation had been expanded exponentially. The Israelis did not respond.

Mary joined me for lunch at school and then we went in to Villiers for a parent-teacher conference. Kate's comments on the teachers were hilarious—and right on target (or "spot on" as they say here.) I think it is a universal truism that no one can do imitations like a kid mimicking a teacher.

After dinner and some early evening reading, Kate went to bed and we walked up to Finnegan's. For the first time since we arrived almost five months ago, some drunk bothered me. He was not antagonistic to me—as a Yank—but he gave a lot of grief to John McGinn, who is with the University's administrative office and who is from Omagh in the North. Called him a "Brit" and several other things. John is a gentle person, and I was offended for him. I told the guy I didn't know how long it took him to get in the place, but it was going to take him about ten seconds to leave and pointed to the front window. To my amazement (and relief), he stared at me, excused himself and left. Whew!

Saturday, January 19. It was a beautiful spring-like morning. Puffy clouds drifted across an azure sky. The news was not so serene, though. Iraq had attacked Israel again—with SCUDS—and Israel was on the verge of retaliation. Pretty tense stuff. After four thousand sorties against Iraq, the Allies appeared to be no closer to taking Kuwait back from them. It still promises to be long and bloody in my judgment.

I took Kate up to Ashroe and she rode "Wallace." The horse was recalcitrant but Kate was persistent. She kicked him into trotting, log-jumping and semi-cantering. While her trainer was pleased, Kate was mad because she felt she hadn't adequately commanded "Wallace." She's doing well. Her posture is good, and her confidence is great.

I had a pile of things to do at school later, including more work on International Relations. I organized next week's schedule, at least on paper.

Sunday, January 20. It was overcast, with some "misting" this morning. Rather like an early spring day at home, in the upper forties. I couldn't help but flash back to a freezing cold January 20th thirty years ago when "Moose" McBride and I shinnied up the scaffolding that held the television camera bank in front of JFK's Inaugural stand.

It had been bitter cold that morning and the wind was like a razor. My legs got severely scraped as I climbed. The blood congealed and stuck to my pants, then tore loose, reopening the scabs. But our Man on the White Horse was about to become President of the United States, and I didn't feel one single pain. ("Moose" is now Professor Edward J. McBride, Chairman of the Department of Politics at the University of Halifax in Nova Scotia.)

I rode in to Ryan's for the papers. God, were they bleak! The London Sunday Times would have one believe that the American leadership had been lying outright about our capacity, our successes, and our losses. It sounded as though Bush has gone too far to cut any deals.

One story in the paper made me especially nervous. It was an advisory issued to American citizens by our Embassy in Dublin. Watch out. Any suspicious moves around one's house, school or workplace, or notice of anyone who appears to be observing us should be reported to the Gardai immediately. There are several thousand Iraqis living in England and France with free access to the rest of Europe including Shannon Airport and environs.

The Embassy emphasized that Americans are somewhat vulnerable to attacks and (implicitly) to kidnapping. Reading that was like swallowing a bottle of paranoia pills. It resurrected all the instinctive fears I had somewhat suppressed earlier in the week. To add fuel to the fire, a group of kids I had never seen before showed up at the front door. Kate had met some of them at O'Reilly's video shop. Their expressed purpose was to see where the Yanks lived. Just great!

We went to the 5:15 at the Jesuit Church

After a quiet dinner, we settled in for more reading and occasional newsbreaks. If we had a TV, I know the damn thing would be on twenty-four hours a day at this point. Glad we didn't succumb.

We went to bed about 11:00, but I kept hearing vans and trucks drive by and slow down out in front. I even heard voices in front and back of the house. Who's afraid of Baby Jane?

Monday, January 21. I walked Kate up to the bus, trying to manifest complete composure. The situation in the Gulf was murky, with Allied airmen being paraded in front of the cameras reading phony statements, and questions being raised about our capacity to inflict really serious military damage.

I spent most of the day at school sorting out and reviewing lecture materials, and I completed an initial bibliography for the American Studies reference library.

Before retiring, I read more of Will Durant's "Age of Truth" for several hours. During the night I heard a banging on the front door. I sat bolt upright. It was those same kidnappers who had been there last night.

Tuesday, January 22. This morning, I wrote and handled some bookkeeping chores at home. I went in to school and finished the bibliography for International Relations. The lectures on American Foreign Policy are looking good at this point.

Wednesday, January 23. More savage attacks on Israel, although they still have refused to respond.

I wrote most of the day—twenty five hundred words worth. The first lecture is coming together nicely.

Thursday, January 24. I took my International Relations notes down to the Departmental office to be typed and then met with Nick Rees. We structured a two-hour program on the flow of events leading up to the Vietnam War, which he wants me to do for his fourth year students. It promises to be an exciting intellectual task from my standpoint.

Friday, January 25. The sun was a fiery ball as I sat in the kitchen in the early morning. "Red sun at dawn, sailors be warned . . . "

Kate actually asked me to walk her to the Dublin Road this morning. For some reason, her mates were not going to be there, and she was just a touch concerned about her security. She's not afraid, just cautious, and that's okay with me.

I picked up my International Relations notes (with a sigh of relief, I might add) and proceeded to accomplish a dozen errands around the campus.

The University gave me clearance today to do student co-op visits and I look forward to seeing some of the countryside. Under the current academic system, all University students take a six-month co-operative education job outside the school in their second and fourth years. The jobs, of course, are academically related and presumably experiential. Each student must be visited on the jobsite by a faculty member. Both the students and the employers are interviewed and the interviews become a part of the students' academic records. It is a novel and worthwhile program.

Mary and Kate were doing "busy" work in the evening, so I went back to school for a concert by the London Winds. It was exquisite. They played two pieces. Beethoven's Seventh Symphony in A Major was absolutely magnificent. Interestingly, the audience did not stand at the end. The sat and applauded—vigorously—but not one person stood up as they would have in the States. The second work sent me up to the ceiling. It was Mozart's Serenade in B Flat, the "Gran Pastita." Seven movements. The vibrancy and precision were thrilling.

Saturday, January 26. There was a very heavy frost this morning. It was quite cold, but the red sun was up again and the sky was crystal clear. I wrote and took down incidental notes for my next lecture. Mary and Kate went up to Ashroe.

Kate rode "Wallace" again, but she said today he was sprightly and responsive. She cantered well several times, was able to slow him to a trot, then a walk, and then to speed him up again. She felt great.

I think they will get into serious jumping next week, although Kate told me she almost involuntarily jumped this morning during one of the "gear shifts." Scared me to think about it.

I measured the fuel oil before we left. Still have six hundred liters out of fifteen hundred and five at the beginning of October. We're conserving. Hope to make it through March without another purchase.

It was a beautiful day, so Mary and I went for a walk in the direction of the Dublin Road. A woman in a car stopped to enquire where she might find the house of Madame Visan, a fortuneteller. That was a first for us, although I understand there are quite a number of people throughout Ireland who regularly patronize fortunetellers, conjurers, and the like. There are a variety of Druid-like influences still alive in this society.

As we were walking back by the fairy fort, Sean and Margaret Jackson, neighbors down our road, drove by and invited us to stop for tea. They have a very old but thoroughly modernized cottage called "Clyduff" (Black Ditch). Their end of the road is only a little over a lane wide and is flanked by thousands of brambles and fruit trees.

Margaret is the spitting image of a young Katherine Hepburn. Even sounds like her. She is very British. Sean is Irish but was raised in England and sounds British. The kids all speak with Limerick brogues!

There was a fellow plodding through our backyard when we got home. He was carrying a shotgun and had a hunting dog. Gave a friendly wave when he spotted me in the window and went on chasing whatever he was after. Nobody seems to stand on much ceremony here.

Sunday, January 27. The 7:00 a.m. news said there had been a terrible oil spill in the Persian Gulf that is wreaking all sorts of ecological havoc.

After breakfast, we went to the 11:00 Mass at Ahane. Not too crowded, so we had an opportunity to see and listen to many of the people. It was a throwback to my youth again. All those farmers with their weather-beaten faces and dark caps; those plump ladies with sparkling eyes and innocent laughter. It was a treat.

Fr. Minogue, who makes a very dour appearance from the altar, dropped by the house unexpectedly. He was a peach. Kept telling us how much he loved tea, but his red nose told me he liked something stronger as well. He was very witty and impish. Pure white hair, ruddy complexion, rimless glasses, broad smile, and jutting jaw. About sixty-five, I would have guessed. He told some funny church stories: "God was a woman, until she changed her mind."

He had come by to meet us preparatory to Kate joining the Confirmation class. I think he felt good when he left. He took a look at the "lesson book" and said with a twinkle in his eye, "Have Kate learn this and it'll be all the theology she'll ever need."

Monday, January 28. As soon as I reached school I went in to pick up my typed notes. Wanted to do a final editing. Frankly, I was a little nervous about a major American foreign policy lecture. Suppose I ran into a broadside on the Gulf? What if they hit me on Vietnam? Or Nicaragua? What if...?

I had a pleasant surprise in the mail—a note from Tip O'Neill congratulating me on what I was doing here at the University. He said he just got out of the hospital after a bad bout with pneumonia. He and Millie were heading south for the winter.

My classroom was in use until well after the hour, so I didn't get a chance to scan the place beforehand. When I walked in, there was no lectern and no lamp to use with the notes. Instead I had to stand behind a small desk and try to glance at my notes from a couple of feet away, which was next to impossible. I decided to "wing it." I ad libbed for about fifty to fifty-five minutes. They were a good class—about thirty of them. We broke for coffee (it was a two-hour lecture) and one of the students who had been with us at Thanksgiving dinner walked up and said he heard that I was taking a "real liberal" approach to the Gulf conflict. I asked what he meant. He said he heard that I had questioned why we were there. This was apparently a "liberal approach." He not only supported the Bush initiative, but refused to even question it. I explained that I would not publicly challenge Bush, but that personally I thought the policy of propping up a dictatorship like Kuwait was a disaster.

It suddenly dawned on me that yet another generation is being swept up in the patriotic fever—a generation which has known no wars and very little privation. It's cruel what the world will do to them in a few short years. The young man did offer a hint of reality, however. Said he wasn't sure now whether he'd join the Coast Guard after graduation. I smiled and said nothing.

The second half of the lecture went very smoothly. We got into policy questions and U.S. strategy, 1945-1985. They were responsive.

Tuesday, January 29. As I walked Kate up to the bus, I noticed a heavy fog along the horizon. It formed an odd pattern, following the River Mulcair down to the Shannon.

There was an eerie sensation, as though the river itself were bubbling over. It created a sinewy, misty path snaking through the air just above the treetops.

There was a funny scene in the school Close (quadrangle). Half a dozen guys were pulling a portable stand around. It had all sorts of posters on it and obviously had something to do with student activities. They were singing and laughing and jeering at the girls in the vicinity. At one point they formed a chorus line on the lip of the fountain-pool and began a "Rockettes" number. Two girls came running up from behind and shoved the first two guys in the line. Like dominoes (or Busby Berkeley girls) the heroes went into the pool seriatim. There was a roar of approval from the girls on the sideline. The guys chased the two girls and caught one. In she went. This time it was the lads who roared from the sideline. There was a timeless air about the whole episode.

Wednesday, January 30. This was mostly a day full of "busy" work, phone calls, correspondence, etc.

While trying to make a long distance phone call for me, the switchboard operator told me several Marines had been killed earlier. This is it, I thought. I went over to the Stables and stood, glued to the TV until 7:00.

Thursday, January 31. The radio announcer reminded his audience that this was the one hundred ninth anniversary of FDR's birth. How well I remember the annual March of Dimes Dinner in Syracuse on this date. My uncle, Dan Gorman, had been chairman of the event for years. President Roosevelt had been the motivating force behind the war on polio and the birthday dinners served as major fundraisers in the effort across the country.

After Kate left for school, Mary and I made a quick run over to the Heritage Center in Tipperary town. I had talked with the Director of the Center on the phone and had given her some preliminary information on my father's family. She had tentatively identified a person we thought might have been my great-grandfather. Unfortunately, the lead proved false.

Mary dropped me back at school and I did some more research on Vietnam. Nick Rees came by and we worked out the plans for our joint lecture on Monday.

The six o'clock news was very grim. Active ground fighting on a widespread front.

Kate was up to her neck in homework, so we had a quick dinner. She then went to the den and Mary and I went in to the Church/State series.

It was an interesting session with a Romanian Orthodox priest as guest speaker. He spoke on the East-West split in Christianity, the development of a vulgate theology in the Eastern (Byzantine) Church, and an intellectual and structural approach in the Western (Roman) Church. It was my first real exposure to the distinctions and I found it intriguing.

Friday, February 1. Kate and I walked up to the bus, but had to watch our step. The road was covered with 'black ice,' a treacherous, almost imperceptible glaze on the surface. Because it is patchy and because it is practically invisible, it causes thousands of accidents every year, both pedestrian and vehicular.

I had a long lunch with John Coakley, whom I have humorously dubbed "My Leader—the Archbishop of Claremorris" (his hometown in County Mayo). John is a very scholarly man, despite his impish and iconoclastic proclivities. And he knows the flow of domestic politics. We discussed the infrastructure of the Irish political system. It was a fascinating and enlightening conversation.

I am becoming more and more intrigued by the subtleties and nuances of politics here. Since there is no great ideological divide, the underpinnings of the parties are more difficult for an outsider to fathom. Personalities, historical references, and regionalism play a role, to be sure, but the political landscape here simply couldn't be framed in an American matrix. As I get to know the people better, I'm sure I will understand their politics better.

Saturday, February 2. I drove Kate up to Ashroe this morning. She rode "Wallace" again, and he was a bit recalcitrant. The instructor switched her to "Andy" to canter. Kate really didn't appreciate that and so she didn't quite get to the next plateau—jumping— today.

I drove in to school in the afternoon and came across an Irish phenomenon. Several sheep had broken through a fence on the Dublin Road and wandered onto the highway. It caused confusion, chaos, and a traffic jam. I thought it was hilarious. Back in the States, I probably would have come unglued and spent the waiting time leaning feverishly on the horn. Instead I just sat back and laughed.

That evening the three of us went up to Killaloe to a dinner party. On the way home we were stopped at a Garda roadblock. Predictably, they were accosting traffic at a hairpin curve in the road ("one never knows what's just around the corner on an Irish road..."). They were "bagging" drivers, making them blow into a special bag to measure alcohol on their breath. I rolled down the window very casually and the Gard said, "And who have we here?" I told him, and he wanted to know where I lived.

My gut response was, "Washington, D.C."

"Here on holidays, are ye?"

"Yes, sir."

"Thank you."

"Thank you, SIR."

Mary was very proud of the finesse. Even said to Kate as we drove away, "Did you hear him?" Kate laughed.

Sunday, February 3. I went over to school and spent several hours working on my next lecture. We went in to the Jesuit Church and then loafed around the house, reading and grazing. It was a lazy, rainy evening.

Monday, February 4. I finished my thoughts on the lecture, and Mary drove me in to the University. There was an invitation to speak at University College of Dublin waiting for me. It had come from Michael Holmes, a bright young faculty member at UCC whom I had met when I attended the Political Studies Conference in Cork last October. Of course, I will accept his offer.

The lecture went smashingly well. Nick opened with a crisp, clinical approach to Vietnam. I followed up with an hour of ad lib commentary on the various dimensions of U.S. involvement. I took the students through thirty years of American commitment, citing both internal and external aspects of the political, social, cultural, and economic forces that shaped the involvement.

The students applauded enthusiastically when I finished. Nick stopped by the office later. I could tell he was very pleased. It was <u>his</u> course, and he had been able to provide <u>his</u> students with an American perspective, something never attempted before at the University. It was a good day for both of us.

Tuesday, February 5. It was absolutely raw out there today—really dank and windy.

Called Michael Holmes in Dublin to accept. He asked me to lecture on Monday, February 25. Maybe we'll go up on Sunday and stay over.

There was some good feedback on yesterday's program. Always nice to hear.

Wednesday, February 6. Today was almost a "zero" on the charts for me, but Mary had a fairly productive day. She went in to Moyross, one of the poverty neighborhoods in Limerick City. I went off to a Faculty Board meeting at school.

Mary is getting involved in early childhood play programs and in exposing poor mothers to many of the advances made in pre-kindergarten education. It is really fertile ground here for her as a professional.

I sat like a lump through hour after agonizing hour of the faculty session.

Anyway, at least one of us had a good productive day.

Thursday, February 7. The whole family slept until 7:30 this morning, which was inordinately late for us. Kate made some of the fastest moves of her young life. She was up, dressed, fed, and packed by 7:40, and I drove her to the bus. I hoped she had washed her face and put her socks on. In any event, she made the bus, which is, no doubt, the social highlight of her day.

I came back and measured the fuel oil again. About six hundred and twenty-five liters. Very good conservation, considering the weather. We've closed off several rooms of the house. Everyone in Ireland does. It would cost a fortune otherwise. We have a huge living room, a very large dining room, a big den, a two-story hallway, a divided kitchen (food preparation in one area, dining in the other), and a bathroom on the first floor. The second floor has three large bedrooms and a master bedroom, a walk-in linen closet and two full bathrooms. The ceilings throughout the house are ten feet. The place is heated by radiators.

Even with some areas closed we have plenty of warm rooms – and lots of comfortable sweaters. I think maybe we can make it to April without more fuel. We've all been cold on a regular basis (Ireland's weather is bone-chilling in the winter because of the dampness and the wind) but we haven't had colds. Drink gallons of citrus. We're surviving okay.

I had a long chat with Nick Rees and his graduate assistant, Adele Clancy, about the International Relations course. It is taking good shape now. We discussed ways in which it could be beefed up with more emphasis on case studies and a tighter relationship between the cases and the theory. Nick said, "They're going to get the theory whether they like it or not," and of course he's right.

Nabil Adawy called this afternoon and asked if I would be interested in teaching International Relations to his graduate students in the fall. While I knew it was not my longest academic suit, I said I would be happy to get involved. I'd love the challenge, particularly if it included an American option, which I am already slowly developing at the undergraduate level.

He is now scheduled to meet with the Dean and the President to see what can what can be worked out.

After dinner, Mary and I came back in to the Church/State series and it was magnificent. A Pastor Prusser, minister to the 800-1000 German Lutherans in Ireland, lectured on the Churches in Nazi Germany—especially the role played by Dietrich Bonhoffer, the noted Lutheran theologian. It was a fascinating program by someone who had grown up in the Third Reich. He told how half the Lutheran Church became the Established Church, supporting the Nazis, the other half the Confessing Church, which rejected and opposed Hitler. He also spoke in somewhat anguished tones of the Concordat signed between the Vatican and Berlin, which left each to its own functions. The series continues to be very impressive.

Friday, February 8. We were all up a little after six this morning. I insisted that Kate shower before dressing. She's beginning to act like so many of the kids here who shower once a month whether they need it or not. Actually, body odor is very commonplace and, I think, quite acceptable in Ireland and throughout much of Europe. Most Americans, though, feel almost unnatural unless swathed in lilac scents and reeking of rose water and baby powder. In any event, it's one of the cultural differences I haven't come to grips with yet.

I went over to the bank to do a little business this morning and the shock of the exchange rate almost knocked me over—$1.84 to the pound. That war in the Middle East has almost sunk the dollar. I read where we are spending five hundred million per day – when we're already four trillion dollars in debt. The Central Banks in a half dozen countries had to intervene yesterday to save the dollar from collapsing completely. Who would have believed that in just ten years the American economy could be brought almost to its knees.

Saturday, February 9. After rousing Mary and Kate and seeing them off to Ashroe, I went back to bed. I don't know whether its been the cold air, or the schedule (or just gradual disintegration), but I have been very tired and sleepy this week.

Kate rode "Andy" under great protest. Mary said she cantered six different times. That represents tremendous progress. She was afraid of him because he is rambunctious, but she decided she was going to be the boss. Even stayed with him when he stumbled and nearly fell. She was full of herself when she came home.

I went in to school to write and to pick up some source material for my Dublin lectures.

Sunday, February 10. It was one of those really crisp and clear winter days, and so following Mass, we decided to go for a spin. Kate and her gang were going to make St. Valentine's Day candies and opted out of the tour.

Mary and I headed for nowhere in particular. We drove over through West Limerick and when we saw a sign for Curragh Chase Park, Mary suggested we go see what it was. It turned out to be a spectacular public preserve and park with all sorts of winding paths and roads through a pine forest. There were sylvan species from all over the world (I'm not quite sure how they survive here), and picnic grounds, lakes, trails, and nature walks.

The Estate, which now belongs to the Irish Government, was the home of Aubrey de Vere, the famous Irish poet who, along with many other intellectuals, joined the Catholic Church in the nineteenth century under the influence of Henry Cardinal Newman and the Oxford Movement. The Main House is literally boarded up, either out of neglect, lack of funds or a low ranking on the government's priority list. The grounds are wonderful though. We must go back there when the blossoms are out.

Since it was still early and the day was bright and clear, we decided to wander toward Ballybunnion on the Atlantic Coast in County Kerry. We'd never been to that particular village.

An attorney friend of ours from Washington, D.C., Mike Flaherty, bought a place there a year or so ago. For some reason, I had been under the impression that Ballybunnion was a refined, semi-elegant resort town with a few upscale restaurants and championship golf courses. In fact, it is a swinging burg with dozens of discos, bars, pubs, eateries—as well as refined restaurants and splendid links. It reminded me of a mini-Ocean City, Maryland.

I had no idea where Flaherty lived, but using my old Advanceman techniques, I figured the golf club would know how to reach him. Sure enough, the bartender knew him, knew he wasn't here, knew where he lived, and knew the fellow who knew all the other answers.

Monday, February 11. Cold and overcast this morning, but no precipitation.

Went in to school and spent considerable time re-reading several chapters of Page Smith's *The Nation Comes of Age*. It is a very valuable background sourcework and an anecdotal cornucopia of American history.

I walked into the Stables and there was a phone call from Mary. It was 5:45 and she had not heard from Kate who is always home by 4:30. I flew home—scared to death that all my fears of a couple of weeks ago had come true.

Kate was already home, but she had come in with some cock and bull story about the bus driver not letting them aboard and how they had to wait downtown. Had no idea where a pay phone was.

She had come home with her jacket wadded up in her backpack. I figured they skipped school or just went on a junket. Mary was furious over the jacket because Kate was already sniffling and running a mild fever. It was teary for a while with all sorts of protestations of innocence and demands to "go back home" preferably alone I think.

Tuesday, February 12. Kate said she wanted to leave a little early this morning because she and the boys had agreed to meet at 7:40, hop on the bus as it was going North, get a seat, and then ride back in to town rather than wait for the southbound leg of the trip and have to stand all the way in. It was raining, cold and bleak, but she and I made it by 7:40. At 7:55 the boys still hadn't arrived. The northbound bus had passed us by in the bad visibility, so we walked across the Dublin Road to catch it as it returned from Castelconnell, assuming that the boys wouldn't show at this point. All of a sudden, another bus came down the Murroe Road, turned the corner (it makes the same loop as the bus they all normally ride), and headed north. Of course, all the boys were on it, waving at Kate and hooting wildly. The second bus overtook the first, the boys transferred, and by the time the first bus got back to our stop, they all had seats and Kate had to stand. Her distrust of boys rose measurably. So did mine. I had stood there with her and was soaked to the skin.

Talked with Michael Holmes in Dublin to confirm the 25th of February. I think I'll lecture on the Separation of Powers Doctrine—with a dash of Federalism, time permitting. He said the audience would be mixed: some might have a reasonably sophisticated understanding of the U.S. system, but most would not.

There is no American Studies Program as such at UCD. A course, or two, is offered periodically, and at different levels, but nothing is structured.

We had a traditional Shrove Tuesday dinner—pancakes and sausages.

Wednesday, February 13. This was Ash Wednesday, so we all got up early and went over to the Salesian Church for Mass and ashes.

Today's Departmental meeting ran about three hours and was quite lively. The MA Degree in European Affairs appears to be in trouble internally, the Library budget for the Department (and the College) is in shambles, and there is more than a modest amount of faculty dissention.

The news tonight was full of stories on the civilians who were killed by the U.S. raids in Baghdad. Seems we bombed air raid shelters. Several hundred killed, others injured. The pictures were hideous. Our military claimed the sites were actually all military targets and they didn't know why civilians were there. At the risk of sounding unpatriotic, I am having serious misgivings about my government's capacity to tell the truth about anything any more.

Thursday, February 14. I had a SNAFU at the bank today—a returned check from the States. One of the biggest problems I've had here is keeping my accounts straight. Checks cross in the mail, bank statements arrive at the oddest intervals and sometimes out of sequence, transatlantic wire transfers take anytime from overnight to two weeks, depending on traffic or perhaps whether the bank clerk in Ireland decided to go on vacation in the middle of the transfer. For someone whose accounts have always been almost letter perfect, this can be nightmarish.

Patti Punch and I had lunch today and we were joined by Henry O'Shea, a Benedictine monk (yes, another one) who teaches German at the University, teaches at the Glenstal Abbey school, and is working on his PhD in German at Trinity College.

Henry said Glenstal, which has a magnificent academic reputation, is suffering financially. They need to look to a rich market in order to survive. I suggested America. He asked me to meet with the Abbot to discuss the matter in depth and I agreed to do so.

Late in the afternoon, I walked over to the Stables and bumped into a bunch of my students. They wanted to do a little intellectual tap dancing with me.

I called home about eight times to have Mary pick me up but Kate was obviously on the phone. I finally reached Mary about 7:00. She picked me up about a half hour later, but by then the "boyos" were well on their way. They asked me to join them in a bash at Plassey Village, the student apartment complex across from the campus. I demurred, but they insisted it would be going all night—would I please stop by.

We went home and had dinner, but because of the hour, we missed the Church/State program.

Mary and Kate were totally immersed in a party Kate is throwing next Friday night, so I headed up to Finnegan's. On my way home, the Devil took the steering wheel and drove me to Plassey Village. It was like revisiting my youth except I was the only one sober. I was also the only one there in a jacket and tie. Within minutes, I became a verbal target—as I suspected I would. It was a kick. I felt like Clint Eastwood dusting off every little squirt who wanted to "slap leather." I fired a few forensic howitzers that I thought found their marks, but I'm not sure anyone else even understood them.

Friday, February 15. Mary had an early appointment in town and, since I wasn't ready when it came time for her to leave, I had to cycle in through a rainstorm. That's always a treat.

I was about to walk down to John Stapleton's office for a meeting when the phone rang. It was Nabil Adawy. He was leaving for London in a few minutes. Could I come down for a quick chat? I left a note on John's door and went downstairs.

Nabil stood up and said, "Congratulations. You are now my associate in the Masters Degree Program in International Relations. I just met with the President and he gave me the stamp of approval. It's official, but please keep it under your hat."

John and I went over to the University Club for coffee. He wanted to bounce his proposal for a new course in Public Administration off me and pick my brain on a course name. I gave him a few ideas. It was interesting, though. I had been his student up until today. Now he asked me for my input.

As we were leaving the University Club, a crowd was gathering in the hall. I walked smack into Ed Walsh and Jack Daly (Chairman of the Board of the University and Chairman of the Board of the Shannon Development Corporation). We chatted briefly. Ed joked about how he had been able to get the guy who "ran" Congress to come over and work for the University.

Then as we were parting, he said, "I talked with Nabil. I'm very happy about what you two are putting together."

John's ears fairly flapped, so I had to tell him and swear him to secrecy. He was as excited as I over the prospects.

Mary came in to meet me at the Stables and we spent some time with Colm Croffy who is the President of the Student Union. Unlike the States, the SU Presidency here is a full-time job. A student runs for the post, and if elected, takes a year off from school to operate a huge program that would rival most small companies in volume of business and breadth of activities.

It is an incredible learning experience. The president not only handles the business and social aspects of student affairs, he is the ombudsman with the Administration. He also, by law, sits on the Board of Governors of the University. I believe this is the case in all Irish Universities.

We came home early to oversee Kate's first teen party—about ten boys and girls for a belated Valentine's Day reception. The kids managed to stretch out a 6:30-7:30 gathering to 9:30. I finally drove Kate and all the boys up to Castelconnell. The girls all live right here in the neighborhood.

Saturday, February 16. It was my turn to take Kate to Ashroe this morning. Miserable day out. Kate rode "Isabel," a beautiful roan mare. Big horse, the biggest Kate had ever been on. She had fear (but not panic) written all over her face. She was superb, though. Handled her like a pro. Trotted and cantered and cornered perfectly. I was really proud and her teacher was thrilled. No jumping today—all indoor activities, because of the weather. I told Kate she should ride back in the saddle a little more, that she'd find it more comfortable and would land squarely in the saddle when she "posted." Her current seating is, however, better for her posture. Forces her to sit erect.

Sunday, February 17. Got up around 6:30 to a perfectly gorgeous day. The sunrise was spectacular.

The inter-varsity windsurfing meet was being held at Dromineer on Loch Derg this afternoon, so we decided to go to the 11:00 Mass at Ahane.

We are gradually being accepted as part of the local scenery. People are starting to nod in more than a casual way, and today, several folks actually stopped and spoke. The Irish Nod, incidentally, particularly in the country, is an unusual movement. At first, I thought there was an epidemic of facial tics blanketing the countryside. The acknowledgement consists of a quick, sideward jerk of the head as though one were flinching. Since we have always been used to a quick, short, forward and downward movement of the brow, the Irish Nod takes on a sort of grotesquely comical overtone.

In fact, all three of us, at one time or another, have had to stifle our laughter or avert our faces to keep from insulting someone who has just 'tic'ed us.

I still couldn't get over the socks on the men. They were all decked out in their "Sunday best" suits, with shirt and tie—and chartreuse or baby blue or white socks.

I did a double take going through the back entrance to the University after church. I saw a group of people in athletic outfits, obviously heavily padded. Looked like football uniforms. I slowed down and sure enough there were a couple of helmets and a football lying on the grass. On my way out a few minutes later, my curiosity got the better of me and I stopped. It was a scrub match. Several guys in their twenties wearing Pittsburgh Steelers' uniforms—black and gold—with their names sewn on the backs. I learned they are starting from scratch. Bought their own uniforms and equipment. They were thrilled to meet an American who knew something about the game. There are apparently three other teams in Dublin and Northern Ireland.

I told them I thought some American sponsors might be interested in helping them out. I gave them my card and suggested their coordinator call me. A fellow named—you guessed it–O'Sullivan.

It was a forty-five minute drive up to Dromineer (in North Tipperary), but Martha Laffan, who was going to caravan up with us, knew a back way, a shortcut that took an hour and a half! No problem though. It was sunny with only patchy clouds and no wind—a beautiful day for a drive.

When we got there, some people were stacking their sails on racks and others were disassembling. I couldn't believe the meet was over. There were quite a few Universities, regional colleges, and technological schools entered in the program.

A fellow told me the lake was like a mirror until 2:30—no wind at all—and that they had to call the meet off. They never would have been able to complete all the races before dark. It began to cloud up at that point and suddenly the wind came and the temperature took a pronounced dip. We headed back home.

Monday, February 18. Kate is on mid-term break this week and Mary and I are both doing lots of paperwork, so today turned out to be one of those "I couldn't tell you what I accomplished if my life depended on it" days.

Tuesday, February 19. As Kate and I walked up to the Dublin Road, we noticed some robin-sized birds with speckles. We also saw flowers resembling lilies-of-the-valley. The two spottings helped us to warm up, if only psychologically.

Late in the afternoon, Mary came in to the University and we went to a history seminar with a lecture by John Logan from Thomond College. He spoke on the "Hedgeschools in Ireland." and began with the surreptitious education of Catholics during the Repression. Aside from being denied the right to own property, to hold public office, or to practice their religion freely, Catholics in Ireland were forbidden to attend school, thus the hedgeschools. These "classes" were held in ditches, behind hedgerows, in the hills, almost anywhere the British couldn't find them. Eventually the schools grew into a private education system and, with the "repeal" laws of the early nineteenth century, they became the National schools in 1830.

It was a thoroughly engaging lecture. Logan, incidentally, did his MA in Economic History at Trinity.

Wednesday, February 20. I had an appointment this morning with Noel Mulcahy, the new Vice President for Research. I wanted to discuss an umbrella American Studies program that would cover all the University's various fragmented approaches to the U.S.

Noel is a delightful character and a longtime practicing politician. He is also one of the great 'bob-and-weave' artists around this place (and there are some GREAT ones). I never really got a commitment out of him, but I think he said the program should be left to the Humanities College, and the other people—Business, Engineering, and the University Foundation—would have to do their own things. He has a curious way of bs-ing that sounds substantive—what John Stapleton calls "spurious certitude."

Noel invited me to join him in Dublin next Tuesday for a personal tour of the Oireachtas (the National Legislature). He was a member of the Senate for four years. I'm going to stay over Monday and take him up on the offer. Mary might stay also, particularly if Noel's wife Caroline goes up with him.

I wandered over to a meditation service this afternoon. It was a Zen-inspired program in which everyone was asked to sit and listen to their knees and feel the levitation of the spirit (and presumably the chairs). This was not my cup of tea. I said to someone as we left, "I couldn't concentrate. I kept listening for my capillaries to break."

After a bite to eat, I went to a Faculty Board Meeting. Four hours and forty-five minutes worth. It was incredible but enlightening. Nitpicking, pedantic, bureaucratic, periodically childish, testy, and occasionally intellectual. It was an eye-opener in terms of campus politics.

On one particular issue, the group actually started off with complete agreement and then proceeded to spend over a half hour explaining why they all agreed!

When we got out of the meeting, several of us repaired to the Stables where we rehashed the entire session, but this time with much humor and Guinness.

Thursday, February 21. We were up early to go over Kate's religion course. Fr. Minogue was coming later to quiz her for Confirmation.

I had a coffee meeting with Malachy Glynn at the University Club. Having arrived early, I waited for him at the Club Table with several old insiders. The topic for the day was the Tinkers who had decided to set up camp on the University's doorstep. The image-conscious University administration was, of course, furious, but the table wits were reveling in the hilarity of it all. One fellow said the Tinkers came there because they thought a year at the University would look good on their résumés. Another told how their mail was delivered "c/o University of Limerick." One other fellow, however, related a bit of a horror story. It seems there was a rather high-tone development going up over in Monaleen. Someone bought two of the houses and put down six thousand pounds in cash on each. The developer got suspicious and had his lawyer track down the purchasers, who turned out to represent a trust, which turned out to be a front for the Tinkers. The next day the developer, fearing the ruination of his whole project by the two prospective junkyards in the middle of everything, coughed up sixteen thousand pounds per house to buy them back. Pretty clever racket, and probably legal as well.

Mary picked me up late in the afternoon. We decided not to go to the Church/State gathering. It featured some Irish journalist lecturing on Bishop Romero of El Salvador. I had lived with all that stuff for ten years at home and really wasn't interested.

Friday, February 22. The ground war apparently began this morning, but details here are sketchy. It was not a very productive day although I was quite busy most of the time.

Saturday, February 23. I attended the "Convergence" conference on the European Monetary Union today. The establishment of a single, uniform European currency is one of the most fractious issues confronting the European Community. The fear among many member nations now is that the Bundesbank, on the strength of the German Deutchmark, will absolutely overwhelm the economies of the weaker nations. Of course, it is axiomatic in political, economic, and academic circles that European Integration is impossible without a monetary union.

Sunday, February 24. It was the usual Sunday morning drill. Up early. Ryan's for the papers. And 11:00 at Ahane. We walked to Mass and, as we passed Tommy McNamara's cottage, we saw a riot of orange, purple, and white. The crocuses and snowdrops were out by the hundreds. There were also Chinese lanterns, which had blossomed early. It was beautiful.

After Mass, I drove over to school to pick up some reference works. Rees and Coakley were both plodding away in their respective offices.

I said, "What are you two doing here? It's beautiful out—and warm."

"Where else?" replied Nick.

So much for the scholarly bachelors.

I stopped over at the playing field to watch a Gaelic Football match. The field was sloppy and slippery. The players seemed to revel in it. Tough game. Have no idea who won or what the rules were (although there don't appear to be too many rules—at least observed rules).

"Lauran" was a madhouse that night with Kate packing for a two-day stay at O'Sullivans and Mary and I preparing for a dawn departure to Dublin.

Monday, February 25. I got up about 5:00 and made coffee.

We didn't pass a single car on the way into town. For the most part, Ireland is like a morgue at that hour anyway. It is not a 'morning' country. Even Colbert Station was deserted. I saw the stationmaster and asked where the dining car was. There wasn't any, even though one had been advertised. What about coffee and a danish? No. Nick Rees had warned me. He said breakfast was scheduled on the 7:00 a.m. but it depended on what kind of a weekend everyone had. Apparently no one wanted to put the program together, so there simply was no breakfast service today. Nor was there anything available in the station. Not even a machine.

I walked out to see if there was any kind of coffee shop in the neighborhood. The streets were deserted as well. Dead silent. Not a car. Not a sound. Not a body. I walked over to the Glentworth Hotel.

The kid sweeping the street said the coffee shop wouldn't be open till, "Oh, maybe half after seven (7:30). It's a cup of coffee ye want?"

He disappeared into the kitchen and emerged with a small pot with milk and sugar. I paid him and bought a couple of newspapers for the journey.

As I walked back to the station, I heard church bells ring. I thought it was the 7:00 Angelus and I had missed the train. It was the fifteen-minute warning for Mass somewhere.

We left the station on the dot. Train departures are about the only things that even approximate a scheduled performance in Ireland.

I thought the train would go up the tracks near our house, but we went into Limerick Junction instead. It was very scenic with the sun coming up on the frosted fields that were separated by hedgerows for miles in all directions.

We passed a small forest outside Templemore, and I noticed rust on the tops of the trees. I suspect, even with the Atlantic at her side, that Ireland has at least a modest problem with acid rain.

On through to Port Laoise, Kildare and, finally, into Heuston Station in Dublin at 9:26—one minute off schedule.

Mary was off to an appointment and I went bookstore browsing until Michael Holmes picked me up.

UCD is Southeast of the City Centre. It is a pleasant twenty-minute drive.

Architecturally, the campus is nothing to brag about. It is early post-war Berlin, with drab concrete slabs–completely soulless. But what a spread. Acres and acres of buildings and landscaping.

The lecture was a numerical bust (apparently it had conflicted with several heavy programs on campus), but academically, it was fairly successful and well received.

Because of the size of the group, we sat around a square of tables. I skipped around a good bit. The structure of a formal lecture would have been too rigid for the intimacy of the setting. The leading scholars in the Department of Politics and two Doctoral candidates sat in on the program. I gave the group a solid intellectual constitutional backdrop to the American system and then we proceeded to the nuts and bolts of how it works.

They were fascinated with the flesh of Washington politics and intrigued by the diffusion of powers among the three branches of the U.S. Government. The question and answer period alone lasted almost an hour and a half and only broke up because two of the group had five o'clock appointments.

That night Mary and I walked about ten blocks from our hotel on St. Stephen's Green to a delightful restaurant in Rathmines, a Dublin neighborhood. It was an intimate little place with background music. As we sat down, the system played "Wabash Cannon Ball" and "Them Oklahoma Hills." I roared. Here we were thirty-five hundred miles from home in a candle-lit restaurant and they were playing C & W!

We took a long walk after dinner and then went back to watch television in the room. We still don't have a set at home. The evening's program ended and the network went off the air at 11:52 to be followed by a test pattern. Shades of the U.S. in 1950!

Tuesday, February 26. After breakfast we both left for appointments and agreed to meet at the National Gallery late in the morning.

We spent a delightful couple hours wandering through the collections of Jack Yeats (brother of William Butler Yeats) and John Lavery and then headed for the shopping arcades and lunch in the Grafton Street area.

We met Noel Mulcahy at Buswell's Hotel and proceeded across the street to Leinster House, the seat of the Irish Government (Leinster House is equivalent to the U. S. Capitol Building).

There were no real security measures at Leinster. No electronic doors or detectors. Just a few Gardai without guns. We did have to get visitors' passes, however. It was almost exactly like visiting the U.S. Capitol—thirty years ago.

Noel knew many, many people and was in his glory introducing us. We headed toward the Dail (the House) wing first. As we went up the stairway leading to the gallery, there was a picture of Eamon De Valera addressing a Joint Meeting of Congress in Washington in 1964. When I told Noel that I was in the Chamber at that time and remembered the speech very well, he almost came unglued. De Valera was, of course, "Himself," "Dev," the former President of the Irish Republic, Founding Father, and pinnacle of the Fianna Fail Pantheon—and Mulcahy is a true-blue Soldier of Destiny, a Fianna Fail man down to his toes.

It was "question time" on the floor of the Dail, when all the Cabinet have to be present to respond to questions or charges by members of the opposition parties. It was an ideal time to catch many of the political celebrities, and so Noel took us back downstairs. We met several members of the Cabinet, all three of the Opposition Leaders, and many of the party and legislative functionaries.

After a quick tour of the Seanad (Senate) Chamber -they weren't in session-and a sentimental visit to Noel's old seat, we repaired to the sanctum sanctorum bar in the Dail wing. I told Noel that in the U.S. Congress, a Member of the House or Senate could purchase his/her old office chair upon defeat or retirement. He was so impressed with that tradition he must have stopped at least a half dozen people to tell them.

When we reached the bar, Noel introduced me to Maurice Manning, the Fine Gael Party Leader in the Senate.

Manning said out of the blue, "I understand you spent some time at UCD yesterday."

(This country is too small for comfort!)

We had a great political conversation—street stuff again. It was like the old days, and the juices were running. I told the group that had gathered how I had first met Brian Lenihan in Washington in a setting similar to this twenty-five or thirty years ago and how we became good friends over the years. It was the kind of personal politics insiders love to share.

Wednesday, February 27. In the vernacular of the kids, this morning was "yucky." Kate had a terrible cough and I suggested she stay home. Wednesday is her favorite day at school, however, and she was having none of my logic. I drove her up to the Dublin Road and as we pulled over to wait for the double-decker, it flew past going north. I tried to catch it, but the driver was really hitting the pedal. Kate attempted directions, but I got disoriented in the bad weather. I turned around finally, quite frustrated, and headed back down the Dublin Road hopeful that I hadn't missed the bus completely. We were okay. At least Kate had been out of the rain and the car had been warm all the time. On the other hand, I was reduced to a mass of quivering, exposed nerve endings, having driven about six miles in blinding rain at sixty miles an hour.

In the afternoon, there was a knock on my office door. It was one of my fourth year international relations students. He is from Cork and his father had just died a short time ago. I had told him my door was always open. He said he had come to take me up on that offer. We talked for an hour-just casual conversation. No moaning or groaning. He's a very mature young man. I hope I can be of some use to him.

By nightfall, Kate was down with a raging fever and a hacking cough.

Thursday, February 28. The morning brought good news. The Gulf War was over. I am waiting for the other shoe to fall, but hopeful that it won't. It seems that Saddam can claim victory in that his country wasn't annihilated. Bush can claim victory in that the Iraqis are out of Kuwait and their army is demolished. Israel is now the dominant force in the Middle East, the oil companies are safe for democracy, and the United States is committed to the Gulf for the foreseeable future.

The Church/State program tonight was excellent. It was a dialogue between Terrence Hartley, Benedictine from Glenstal Abbey, and John Longside, a Presbyterian minister now in Kilkenny. Both grew up in Belfast. Both had bitter memories of the tensions and bloodshed there, which they shared in detail with us—and with each other. I sensed that neither fully appreciated until tonight what the other had gone through. The commonality of their experiences was meaningful to everyone in the room.

I raised the question of Ian Paisley, a Presbyterian minister who is also a Member of the British Parliament and a leading force in the sectarian antagonisms. Both speakers agreed that Paisley was a politician first, a bigot next, and a Churchman last. Interestingly, Longside had no use for the Orange Order, the pivot around which Protestant antipathies swirl, and Hartley the monk had no use for the Catholic hierarchy. Very illuminating.

Friday, March 1. The phone rang about 8:00 a.m. It was Niamh O'Sullivan from across the street. She runs a pre-school program out of her house for about twenty kids. This morning, she was desperately ill and wanted to know if Mary could take over for her—in forty-five minutes! Mary was happy to oblige. Early childhood education and pre-school kids are her strengths. We often joke about how she married me because she considered me a "case study."

I had a phone call at school from Ellen Hazelkorn at the Dublin Institute of Technology. The Institute is an affiliated College of Dublin City University, as is Trinity College. Ellen is from Chicago, but has been living in Ireland for several years. I met her last fall at the Political Studies conference in Cork. Today she asked me to come up and lecture on American-style lobbying.

Pat O'Sullivan the sponsor of the fledgling Pittsburgh Steelers (Limerick style) had called me earlier in the week and we had agreed to meet for lunch today. It was an enjoyable get-together. O'Sullivan is fortyish and a real go-getter. The football idea took form because of his interest in the impoverished, unemployed, and angry young men in the Moyross section of the city. This was meant to be their safety valve, but it evolved into something that he, too, is now enthused about. We discussed a half dozen angles, including individual and corporate American sponsorships and the possibility of some sort of direct involvement by the Steelers or the National Football League.

Saturday, March 2. It was quite windy and rainy, although not too cold this morning. Kate still wasn't well enough to go out yet. It was the first lesson she has missed at Ashroe. It's a shame, because she's on a roll there now.

We all spent the better part of the day reading and dozing. Kate finished her French homework after dinner and I think everyone was in bed by 10:30.

Sunday, March 3. The wind was very forceful overnight and so the weather changed even more frequently than usual. I got up at one point and the moon was as bright as could be in a clear sky. When I awoke at seven, the wind was howling and it was pouring. I went out to the shed to turn the heat on. I've never learned how to operate the interior heating mechanism, so we have to go outdoors to turn the heat on and off. That's been a real treat at 6:30 in the morning, when it's minus three degrees Celsius and blowing and snowing.

Riding in to Ryan's, I watched the sky and the blowing clouds and actually calculated how much time I had to cycle in and back before the next shower. I made it. I'm beginning to read some of the crazy weather patterns here. It beats carrying and losing umbrellas.

Mary and Kate were both under the weather, so I walked up to Mass alone. By now the sun was shining and it was fairly warm without the wind.

On the way home, I saw a thorn tree that had been cut back by the County Council. There were a number of medium sized branches, which hadn't been completely severed. I tore one off. It made a great walking stick. At the first opportunity, I'll strip and varnish it.

It was pretty quite around the house. I settled into Will Durant's work on the development of the Scholastic Movement in the thirteenth century.

Monday, March 4. I had lunch with two fellows from the electronics/computer faculty in the Engineering College. As frequently happens around here, we fell into the favorite pastime of psychoanalyzing Ireland, her politics, her Church, etc. We ended with their acknowledging both my "broker theory" and the Irish penchant for sweeping everything under the rug. (The "broker theory" is simple: I believe the Irish people historically have been so passive that they are content to let someone else make their decisions and their judgments for them. The Church decides how they will get to Heaven, and they accept it; the politicians, mostly Fianna Fail, decide how they will be governed, and they accept it; and the GAA, the Gaelic Athletic Association, decides how and what they will play, and they accept that likewise.)

Tuesday, March 5. The sun was out this morning, with the promise of warm weather. I walked Kate up to the bus. It was her first day back and she was pretty excited at seeing her bus-mates.

Spent a good bit of time in the office and then went over to the Library to research all the University Prospectuses (Prospecti?) in both the Republic and Northern Ireland. Not one school has a post-graduate program in American Studies. Some have a few undergraduate courses, which are offered spasmodically and at different year levels (I suppose as the visiting faculty come and go). And some offer no courses at either the graduate or undergraduate levels. In short, the field is wide open.

I realized for the first time that I could craft my proposals out of both my fertile imagination and the current paucity of existing course modules. It presented a great opportunity.

Wednesday, March 6. Mary had a terrible night dripping and tossing with the flu, so she didn't even get to sleep until almost 5:00. Kate and I managed to stumble through the sunrise rituals, though, and then headed off to our respective routines.

I spent a couple hours resourcing the International Relations course. The Library holdings are abysmal. I'll have to get most of the required material either in the States or at the U.N.

Fr. Minogue called and told Kate he wanted her to write an essay on the life of Jesus for next week. I asked her how she was going to approach the subject and started to remind her of the Old Testament prophesies when she interrupted with:

"I probably wouldn't even believe in the guy if it weren't for you and Mom. I'm sorry, but those are my feelings."

I probed a little as to where she came up with that thought, and she said, "I've had my own ideas for some time."

She got modestly argumentative when I said there were many other people who didn't believe in Christ, who had never heard of Christ, and who were very good folks. She took this as condescension toward her Jewish friends. At that point I shut up. This thing was going no place. I only hope this isn't the beginning of eight or nine years of this stuff.

Anyway, the essay will be done—and properly.

Since Mary wasn't up to par, she opted out when Kate and I started to leave for the Jean Monet Theater at the University. We went in to hear the Grieg Trio from Norway. They played two marvelous pieces, one Schubert, the other Mendelssohn. The scherzo by Mendelssohn was magnificent. That was one of his long suits anyway. (I've always loved his scherzo to the *Incidental Music to a Midsummer Night's Dream.*)

The audience was so thrilled with the performance that the trio was called back for three encores.

Thursday, March 7. I accessed the Library network from my own desk computer this morning, trying to gather reference works for international relations. Whatever books I found were at least twenty years old, and the appropriate scholarly journals are non-existent. It's very sad. It's also very frustrating. I've arranged for a number of items myself, but the required budgetary input from the University is not forthcoming, either because of a lack of resources, or a lack of commitment, or perhaps a bit of both.

I received my first co-operative education assignment today. I will be visiting four students in Kerry and Cork. If all goes well, Mary and Kate can go with me and sightsee while I interview the students and their supervisors. Should be fun.

We went in for the Church/State session in the evening. Dr. Richard Lang of University College Galway gave both a historical and contemporary overview of the church's influence on the Irish State. He provided insights into the church, the hierarchy, the political parties. They fed/feed off one another in what is probably the closest thing to a theocracy existing in the Western world today.

He predicted the Irish Church will go the way of the church throughout Europe—very few active participants, but ardent in their beliefs. Certainly that's where things seem headed. The issue has been keenly focused by the anachronistic debate here over prophylactics and divorce. Prophylactics are illegal in Ireland and divorce is unconstitutional.

Friday, March 8. I read some of Kate's essay on Christ this morning. It's very articulate and reasonably mature for a twelve-year-old. She's a thinker, but her peers haven't been taught to think for themselves, so she's going through a lot of personal confusion.

Paddy Doran lectured to the History Seminar this afternoon on the "Wild Geese." The "Wild Geese" were the political, military, social, and to some extent, religious leaders who were driven out of Ireland by the British in the seventeenth and eighteenth centuries. It was a very scholarly paper. He focused not as much on where particular émigrés went, as he did on the circumstances into which they went. He zeroed in on Austria, Prussia, and France.

The emigration actually started well ahead of the 1691 Treaty of Limerick, which mandated a leadership diaspora. It was Protestant as well as Catholic. Many of the emigrants became nobility in

Continental Courts through spurious documents (verified by Irish monks on the Continent). Irish soldiers were not unique at that time in Europe. There was a huge mercenary army floating from country to country and from war to war. For instance, both sides in the Battle of the Boyne (1690) in Ireland were largely Irish recruits who returned to Ireland to fight in two opposing armies, one under William of Orange, the other under King James. And the Hapsburgs of Austria were recruiting up to 10,000 men a year long before the Limerick treaty.

Dr. Doran got into a vivid discourse on the sense of Prussian order and marching cadence (Paddy is a German History scholar). The Romans had marched cadently, but the practice had died out and wasn't reintroduced until Friedrich Wilhelm the Elector.

Throughout all of this, Paddy's lecture was well laced with the names of prominent Irishmen who served as military commanders in almost all of the European armies. Many descendants of the original "Wild Geese" ended up in the American Revolutionary War as well. It was a masterful piece of research.

Saturday, March 9. I took Kate up to Ashroe but it was a fairly uneventful episode. Her trainer had them cantering and trotting but not jumping for some reason.

About 4:00 I went off for a bike ride into Annacotty, then down a back road a mile or so, and finally onto an even narrower lane. It led to an old settlement on the River Mulcair. There were ruins still standing, probably an old mill. There was no bridge, but what I reckoned to be the stone underpinnings of some docks.

There were beautiful rapids at that point and, except for a lone fisherman, not a soul in sight. The roar of the river was the only sound. It was serene.

On my way back up the lane, I saw an old man walking toward me in a greatcoat. I vaguely recognized him (from church, I think). As I got close and nodded to him, I saw his grotesque face. It actually scared me. He was thickset and short and he had the triangular face of a brute, with a long flat forehead, high cheekbones, and an almost uncrowned head. He acknowledged my nod, but did not return the smile. It was eerie. I shiver even now as my mind conjures up that picture. He was the "missing link," in an overcoat, I thought.

Sunday, March 10. As we started to leave for church, I discovered a flat tire on the car. I had noticed that it appeared to be a little soft yesterday. Today it was flat. Since I had no idea how to fix it, I got out the bicycle pump and put air in. I pumped and pumped, but it wouldn't fill up. Then I got some glue (when I found the leak) and plastered the area. Obviously, that didn't work either. I think I'm getting totally addled. At that point, we walked to church and left the tire, the pump, and the glue sitting in the driveway.

When I went in to Ryan's for the papers, I saw my brutish friend from yesterday, bent over to about a forty-five-degree angle, thumbing a ride on the Dublin Road. Someone must have stopped for him, because he was gone on my return five or ten minutes later. He's probably a gentle soul, but he has a face that would scare a banshee!

After lunch, I left with my neighbor Pat O'Sullivan for a hurling match in Bruff, about fifteen to twenty miles south of Limerick. It was a league play, but what is known in the trade as a "friendly match," which meant the results didn't count in the league standings.

Pat told me he would have enjoyed playing soccer as a lad, but there were no teams around. Besides, kids were taught that somehow hurling and Gaelic football made them better Irishmen. To this day, no "foreign sport, "e.g., rugby, non-Gaelic football, soccer, may be played on any GAA pitch (playing field) throughout the country, including the national shrine at Croke Park in Dublin.

He said Irish games were peculiarly Irish. They never start on time.

"If soccer is scheduled at 11:00, the game begins at 11:00. The Irish matches might start at 11:whatever," he said dryly.

The match was set for 3:00. It got off at 3:20—not too bad. It was an absolutely fascinating game. Fast and more than a little frightening. It was my first. I couldn't believe no one was injured. The violence is visible and regular, but defensive strategy and survival instincts are at the fore constantly.

The match had two thirty-minute halves. (The times vary according to the level of league play—up to a maximum of forty minutes.) The pitch is one hundred and eighty yards long and ninety yards wide. That is a minimum, but the size, too, can vary. There are fifteen men per team, with three fullbacks and three halfbacks more or less riveted into zone-play and the rest on free-for-all. One point is scored when it is between the uprights (goalposts) but a goal of three points is scored when it is below the crossbar as well. This particular game ended 3+8 (11) to 11, a tie.

The pace was furious. The hurly (playing stick) is shaped in a wide L—about two feet long with a head (or face) about five inches. It is flat and made of ash. The players slap the sliothar (playball), pick it up off the ground, run balancing it on the hurly, or catch and throw it with their hands. They may not take more than three steps, however, after holding the ball, before they must dispose of it—even if only by balancing it on the hurly. It's like the twenty-four-second rule in American basketball.

The sliothar is made of cork innards, with soft leather outside. It has ridges where a baseball has seams. And it travels like a jai alai ball—fast as hell!

It was a great game to watch. Unfortunately, I was so focused on the action and the pace that I probably missed a lot of the strategy. It seemed to me, though, that most of the play was spontaneous because the ball was constantly in motion, no one knew from one second to the next who had possession, and the ball was apt to travel in four directions in the space of ten seconds. Some of the hurling from the field to the goal was spectacular. Perfectly lofted with precision aim.

One of the interesting sidelights was the audience itself. It was a small crowd. A few wives, girlfriends, and kids—but mostly men -old men in Wellies and suitcoats, middle-aged guys probably headed to a pub when the match was over (the pubs, of course are closed from two to four on Sundays), and young would-be Cup winners. Most of them had hurlys with them. Some were playing off the field, others were swinging the sticks at phantom sliothars, and still others were just leaning on them. They all brought their piece of the action, their piece of the GAA, their piece of Ireland with them. It was a great afternoon for me.

Monday, March 11. Since the car was hors d'combat, I borrowed a ride with PJ Carey who lives across the street. He's with Telecom Eireann, the semi-state Irish telephone monopoly. He told me the whole company works on flextime now, and he noted that their sick days had dropped to almost nil since they went to a flexible schedule. People no longer had to take a day off to do special chores, etc. I'd seen his car around the house at different times of the day, and wondered what the hell he did at Telecom.

Dr. Bernadette Whelan stopped me in the hall and asked if I would participate in the History Seminar series, following on the Hedgeschools, the "Wild Geese," and Nabil Adawy's Middle East paper (tomorrow). Said I'd be glad to. She told me it would have to be after the Easter break. I can pick my own subject. I accepted gladly.

At the request of the Business College, I lectured a group of students from Iona College in New York State today. They are here on an exchange program. The University wanted to take advantage of my years of experience at a lobbyist, and so I spoke on the relationship between the U.S. Government and the business community. They seemed to understand and enjoy the material and I enjoyed the post-lecture banter with some other Americans.

After dinner, Mary, Kate, and I went to a piano concert at the Jean Monet. Dmitri Alexseev, a brilliant artist, did three solo pieces, one from a Mozart Sonata, one from a Chopin Sonata, and the Opus #9 from Schumann's *Carnival*—about twenty-one mini-movements. It was stupendous. He received an amazingly long and enthusiastic ovation, but the audience never stirred from their seats. I don't quite understand.

Kate had hardly demurred when I suggested we go, and she thoroughly enjoyed the performance. She even agreed to venture backstage to say hello to Alexseev, but he had disappeared into his dressing room.

Tuesday, March 12. Mary is co-authoring a paper on Early Childhood Development with Dr. Karen Banks in Washington, so I got up early this morning to assume my role as editor. The piece will be

56

presented in the States, but in a separate agenda. Mary also is going to deliver her portion to a Women's Studies program here at the University on Friday. She's justifiably proud.

It was a beautiful spring day, and I had a little time to kill so I took a short walk along the Shannon.

There were quite a few waders chasing salmon, and a number of the squatters who have small fishing huts along the riverside were out retarring roofs and making general repairs on their simple hideaways.

As I crossed an old footbridge leading over into County Clare, I couldn't help thinking that, without the least bit of fanfare, I had just traversed the borders of two ancient kingdoms.

Nabil's lecture was interesting, but his delivery was somewhat stilted. He had just hand-written the paper the night before so he hadn't committed it to memory, and he lost his place several times. On balance, however, he was superb.

He dealt first with the historical perspective of pan-Arabia, the Muslim Empire, the Crusades, and the Ottoman Empire. In short, he spoke of a proud people who have been subjugated, off and on, for several hundred years, and deeply resent outsiders, including the Turks and other Westerners. Then he dealt with the treachery of World War I and the post-war years, the British deceit, the Balfour years, etc.

The most fascinating part of the lecture for me, however, was the constant internecine warfare on the Arabian Peninsula, and the, as yet, undemarcated borders among most of the states. The Palestinians, who have been kicked around by everybody, are central to peace in the area, he said. He likened them to the pre-war Jews of Europe. They are somewhat rootless and represent the intelligentsia of their region.

Wednesday, March 13. It was dangerously foggy this morning. I walked Kate to the bus as I didn't want her negotiating the Dublin Road in this weather.

I made contact with Brian Lenihan. We're scheduled to meet at Buswell's Hotel in Dublin on the 21st. I also made arrangements to lecture Ellen Hazelkorn's class at the Dublin Institute that morning.

Thursday, March 14. This was a real odds and ends day for me. I was on the go all day long, but other than some computer research, didn't manage to accomplish much.

Mary and I went in for the wrap-up session of the Church/State program. It was basically a rehash of all the wonderful weekly gatherings we had held throughout the year. We made some great friends.

Friday, March 15. I drove out to Shannon Airport for a luncheon date at Guinness Peat Aviation (GPA), the giant aircraft leasing company. As we sat down in the dining room, a vaguely familiar face came into view. The girth of the body didn't match the face, however, so I couldn't identify the guy. But when he turned toward me, we both did double takes. It was my old friend Sean Donlon, the former Irish Ambassador to Washington. I hadn't seen him for at least ten years. He's now retired from the Foreign Service and is serving as a troubleshooter/sales representative for GPA.

Sean joined us for lunch and we exchanged all sorts of political gossip. I told him I'd recently had a note from Tip O'Neill and he said Tip had spent five weeks in Massachusetts General Hospital with a very serious case of pneumonia.

After lunch, we took a tour of the place. GPA grosses two billion pounds per year. They buy/sell or lease/finance planes—then sell the leases themselves to investors. What an operation. Currently, they have about three hundred planes in the air. They're putting up a plant at Shannon to do maintenance work. It will employ over three thousand people in a couple of years. It costs between one and five million dollars just to overhaul an aircraft.

It was a most enlightening day.

Saturday, March 16. I woke up about 5:00 and the front of my head was throbbing. It felt as though someone had laid the flat side of a shovel into my brow. My eyes, my forehead, even my jaw ached. I took some aspirin and went back to bed, but the pain wouldn't abate. By then it was obvious that I had a brain tumor.

Mary took Kate up to Ashroe. I started to cough right after they left. It felt like a feather in my throat. Nothing came up, but then I started to choke. I knew it wasn't food lodged in there, and then I suspected a heart attack. I dropped to my knees and gasped for what seemed an hour. I was afraid I would pass out and then the windpipe would simply shut without the extra hard breathing. Finally something broke—by now I was holding onto the edge of the sink for dear life. There was a burst of phlegm. My sinuses had been leaking so much thick stuff that it had actually clogged the trachea. Never heard of that happening. The headache lessened considerably.

I went in to school to pick up some papers I planned to take on my co-op trip Tuesday. Never told Mary about the choking incident. No point in upsetting her.

Sunday, March 17. St. Patrick's morning and a beautiful day. Sunny, with drifting clouds —and warming up.

We went in to the 10:30 Mass at the Jesuit Church. The church is in the staging area for the parade, and the parade was scheduled to start at 11:00. It was an Irish Mass. The sermon was as good as anything I've heard in English. As a matter of fact, it made more sense than most I have heard here. The Credo was sung in Latin in Gregorian Chant. Mary and I both sang. It all came back.

We walked a block or two down O'Connell Street to the parade. It was great. Over a hundred units. We knew dozens of people from all different parts of the city and the society. Felt as though we belonged. Someone told us the Limerick Parade is only about ten years old. Said St. Patrick's Day had been a very religious and very patriotic occasion until recently. The pubs were closed, and most of the day was spent in religious festivities, folk songs, dancing, and storytelling. Even with modern intrusions, the Day is still relatively subdued when compared to its cousins in New York, Boston, or Savannah.

Monday, March 18. We had planned to go in to the Band Parade today, but it was pouring and everyone slept in. In recent years, bands from all over the world, but principally from the States, began coming to various Irish cities to march and compete. It's a bank holiday in Ireland so a good public turnout is pretty much guaranteed—weather permitting.

Kate didn't feel all that well, so we stayed home and played some games in front of the hearth. In the evening she became more and more congested and it looked as though I would be going on my co-op trip alone. Rats! I really wanted them to go with me.

Tuesday, March 19. I left for Cork around 8:00. It was a lovely drive down. Good weather, and since I took the back roads, almost no traffic. (I've actually been here long enough to know some of the back roads.)

I had no trouble covering the sixty miles to Cork City, but I wasn't in the town ten minutes when I screwed up. I ended up going the wrong way on a one-way main thoroughfare. Scared the hell out of about eight drivers, including myself. After one stop for directions, I made my way directly to the County Council without a hitch.

All in all, I did ten interviews during the day—six students and four supervisors. I left about four o'clock. Fortunately, I could continue right out the Western Road, so I didn't have to go back into town in the middle of the evening traffic. Cork is the second largest city in Ireland. I think there are about one hundred thousand people in the city and probably another hundred thousand in the environs, so traffic is a real issue.

The trip through the River Lee Valley was serene. I was surprised at the palaces adorning the hillside overlooking the river. Obviously, there is lots of old, old money in Cork. The city celebrated its eight-hundredth anniversary a few years ago.

I made my way up through the village of Macroom. (Five years ago, Mary, Kate, my mother, and I had stopped here and watched the army guard a bank delivery because of a rash of IRA heists.) From Macroom, I headed up into the mountains. The last two times I was there, it had rained or snowed.

This time it was crystal clear, and the mountains were frightening; they are so savage and wild. It takes a particular breed of people to live in this part of the country. The roads are "Z"-shaped and largely unmarked. I averaged about twenty-eight to thirty mph. The stark beauty of the place is almost overpowering. If Mary and Kate were with me, I would have stopped. The views were breathtaking.

I caught a few showers on the decline toward Killarney, but no really bad weather.

Pulled into Tralee around 5:30 and checked in at the Mt. Brandon Hotel. The one thing I wanted to see in Tralee was the Siamsa Tire', the Irish Folk Theater, so after dinner, I had the desk clerk make the arrangements. He produced a perfect seat—ninth row, middle of the theater (a stereo theater with three stages). It was a celebration of Irish rural life revolving around the blacksmith shop a hundred years ago. Very rich in symbolism. The music was surreal and the dancing (Kerry Steps) was out of this world. Unfortunately, the lyrics (and dialogue such as there was) were in Irish. I'm sure I lost a lot of the flavor, but for six pounds, it was still a bargain.

Wednesday, March 20. Hoping to get home at a decent hour, I got an early start and wrapped up my interviews at the Kerry Council a little after ten. Then, in what must have been a filial reflex, I decided I knew a shortcut out of town and proceeded merrily on my way. (My father, God be good to him, knew a shortcut in every town he'd <u>never</u> been in before.) One hour and six unplanned shortcuts later, I found myself finally on the road back to Limerick. I was pretty ticked-off at myself, but at least I knew my father was proud of me.

Thursday, March 21. I was up early, had a good breakfast and got to Colbert Station in plenty of time to catch the 8:30 to Dublin. The train left right on time.

It was a beautiful sunny day and the countryside through the Midlands looked as though it had been lifted right out of a travelogue. The fields are very green now, and the sheep and cattle are out in force. The sun was warm through the windows as we whisked along northeastward.

On arrival, I grabbed a cab over to the College of Commerce in Rathmines. The College is one of five schools associated with the Dublin Institute of Technology, which, for some archaic reason, awards its degrees through Trinity College.

The lecture went very well. I spoke for about an hour and then threw the program open to an avalanche of questions. I guess I should have anticipated the level of inquisitiveness because of both the subject matter (lobbying, Washington style) and the fact that these students, coming from a parliamentary system, knew almost nothing about the U.S. legislative process.

It was a mild day with intermittent clouds, so I decided to walk the mile or so to my luncheon appointment with Brian Lenihan.

When I reached Buswell's Hotel, the desk clerk informed me that Brian had just called and said he was held up on the floor for a series of votes. Could I call him back at three o'clock? (Even though Brian had lost the presidential election last November, he was still a member of the Dail.) Knowing full well from personal experience how these situations work, I realized that I could end up sitting around all day waiting for a 'window' in the legislative schedule. I had the clerk call his office back and postpone lunch to a more convenient date, and then I left for the train station.

I walked down to the River Liffey and turned west along the quays toward Heuston Station. It's a shame the way the city leaders have let that area go to ruin. It's a "natural" as a tourist attraction, but it's a bit like the derelict inner cities in the States—the real estate promoters have their interests tied up elsewhere. There are some incredibly beautiful and historically important pieces of architecture along the way. Apparently, the 'right' people don't own the properties or they would have been redeveloped ages ago. Said he, cynically.

(Editors Note): In recent years, a master plan has been developed for the Liffey Docklands and the Temple Bar District. The area has gone through a massive upscale transformation not unlike Times Square.

Friday, March 22. I went in to school to do some odd jobs. This is exam week, so most of the faculty is keeping a low profile. It's a good week to wrap up a lot of outside chores.

I fumbled with the computer system for the better part of the day. I'm educating myself on the operation of a PC, and I'm also trying to learn how to do e-mail to American universities through BITNET. Talk about teaching an old dog new tricks! This is like teaching an old dog how to moo!

Saturday, March 23. This was not a particularly productive day. I spent part of it pulling together all the necessary papers for the Internal Revenue Service. Even living three thousand miles from home, without an income, it's heartening to know that the loving hand of one's government is really only as far away as one's wallet.

Since Kate and Mary were both on medication, we cancelled out on Ashroe. It was pretty quiet all day.

Sunday, March 24. We had one of those absolutely beautiful Irish spring mornings today. It was practically cloudless, and pleasantly warm.

I rode in to Ryan's and stopped at the River Mulcair a few hundred yards from the shop. The lads from the area were all out on the banks, fishing poles in hand. I suspected they would be there, so I had brought along my camera. The riversides were lined with anglers, tents, turf fires with coffee pots in them, dogs running and yapping. Young men, old men, and kids were on the shore and in midstream. It was an Irish "L'Sacre' du printemps."

During the day, there must have been twenty kids who stopped by to see Kate—mostly little ones who adore her. Even the boys in the neighborhood, though, have accepted her as an equal now. She plays soccer and has for several years. Her teammates back in Virginia called her "Ironfoot." The boys here are quite impressed. I don't think the feeling is mutual, however, and that's just fine. Said the father.

The neighbors were all out—walking, playing with kids, washing cars, mowing lawns, talking over fences. It was the Universal Suburbia.

Mary and I decided to go for a drive and headed off toward an area in town we'd never visited called Corbally, which is in the shadow of St. Mary's Cathedral. We drove past St. Munchin's Diocesan College and all of a sudden we were in the country at the foot of the Clare Hills. It was beautiful but desolate territory—within a few minutes of downtown Limerick.

We got onto a side road that was rutted, Z-turned and frighteningly narrow. Almost no traffic, but each time a car came toward us, it was a major confrontation—backing up, barely avoiding foot-deep ditches, etc.

We went north over the mountains, then doubled back to a good road that aimed us south again. It led through a pass in the hills. My God, it was spectacular! It provided a vista all the way from Limerick to the Shannon estuary—a distance of perhaps fifty miles. Fortunately we brought the binoculars.

We wound around the hills and eventually arrived back in Limerick in the Moyross section, where Mary volunteers each week with Niamh O'Sullivan. It is your basic slum. Broken glass all over the streets, dirty kids, trash in the yards, broken down cars (at least we could identify with <u>those</u>), even a kid leading a horse through the neighborhood. Pretty depressing. These areas are called Council Housing in Ireland (in all the British Isles far that matter). They're the Irish equivalent of Public Housing projects in the States. I guess there's quite a stigma attached to growing up in one of them. Getting out is very difficult. There is still a real, although increasingly fragile, class distinction in Irish society.

We headed up to "toney" Perry Square. It is an elegantly landscaped park in the center of town, surrounded by expensive 'flats' in neat red brick townhouses. The buildings are all set off with brightly painted Dublin doors. The area is literally not more than five minutes from Moyross but it might as well be on another planet.

The People's Park in the Square was delightful. Forsythia bushes, bleeding hearts, daffodils, primroses, daisies, tulips, hyacinths, all in bloom. The lawns were a rich green and well manicured.

Sacred Heart is just around the corner, and since it was already after five, we walked over to Mass. Paddy Tyrell met us at the door.

The Gospel reading today, of course, was the Passion of Christ. I couldn't help reflecting on those days as a kid when the priest read the long Passion and we were taught not to move—to offer it up. If we didn't move, or scratch, or shift haunches, we'd get a plenary indulgence. Today there weren't even any palms, even though it was Palm Sunday. Instead, the ushers handed out sprigs of indigenous cedar bushes.

Monday, March 25. Villiers was about the only school open today, and since most of the kids from Lisnagry go elsewhere, no bus was available, and I had to drive Kate in to the city.

The University is pretty quiet during the Easter recess, so there were very few people and almost no services available on campus. I stuck my head in the Foundation office. Malachy Glynn, who has resigned as CEO of the Foundation pending a successor, has gone back to the States. I think many people around here were surprised that I did not apply for the position. Most thought I was a natural for it and assumed I would want it. Frankly, I told everyone I was sick of airports, one-night hotel rooms, receptions, conferences, etc. Thirty years of that lifestyle in politics was enough. I might have been interested in planning and directing, but the legwork has no appeal whatsoever. In any event, the job is still open, even after several interviews.

Jerry Cronin, my pal from the cooperative education office, gave me a lift home. There were about fifteen kids in the backyard when we arrived—playing baseball! Kate had suggested it and the boys loved it. It involved running and hitting, the mainstays of teenage boys. The girls were good, too, but mostly giggly. It was a real "scrub" game, played with about a sixteen-inch bat, a green tennis ball, and two gloves. They dug up whatever they could find for the bases. When the kids couldn't throw one another out, they threw the ball at the runner. A novel approach, but no one minded. Kate was thrilled because she was the "hostess," and it was her game.

Tuesday, March 26. I had to arm-wrestle Kate out of bed to take a shower. After phys. ed. at school yesterday and a baseball game last night, I thought she just might need one. She's taking on some of the local cultural habits. B.O. seems to be an acceptable feature of everyday life here—even among people who wear pretty dresses or shirts and ties. Among kids, it is almost a badge of honor. I always thought teenage girls spent about half their time in the shower!

I had set up an appointment with Ed Walsh earlier in the day, and at 3:30 I went over to the President's Office in Plassey House.

Ed was in a taut meeting with Colm Croffy, the President of the Student Union. Colm had led a massive sit-in protesting conditions in the Library. The students have an abundantly legitimate gripe.

On Colm's departure, we got right to the point of my visit.

I told Ed I loved what I was doing, and was most anxious to expand my activities in the International Relations venture with Nabil Adawy, but up to this point the entire effort had come out of my own pocket. I simply couldn't continue without a commitment from the University. He was flabbergasted to learn that I was not being paid. I told him I wasn't there crying—just explaining that I had already spent a ton and couldn't do any more.

For his part, Ed gave me a great deal of moral support, but no specific commitment. He did mention that it was his understanding that the International Relations program would be financially self-sustaining, based on tuitions. That was a new wrinkle, and threw me a little.

Father Minogue was at the house when I arrived home. He was there for Kate's Confirmation program. (The notion of the parish priest actually coming to someone's home for instructions was mind-boggling for our neighbors, but there he was.) I couldn't believe Kate. She dazzled him with BS, and pulled stuff out of her hat. Minogue is a very gentle man—witty and sparkly—but he looks like one who shouldn't be crossed. I held my breath. He responded warmly.

Wednesday, March 27. Mary and I were both up before dawn. Each of us had a lot of research and writing to do. Kate started holidays today, so she didn't even stir until 10:30. I finally left for school, Mary went in to Moyross for her weekly project, and we left Kate with a calendar of chores.

After a reasonably productive day, I stopped over at the Stables to catch some of the playoff matches for the World Soccer Cup. Northern Ireland got blown out of the water by Yugoslavia, to no one's surprise. The big upset occurred, however, when Ireland played England to a tie. The place was mobbed and the crowd delirious. It was a fantastic victory for Ireland.

Thursday, March 28. There was a meeting of the University's Governing Board today and it proved to be quite rancorous. At one point, a very conservative faculty member offered a motion condemning the students for the Library protest march. It carried overwhelmingly. Sad. Sure doesn't give the University a very enlightened reputation. The Library is in shambles. Kids have to wait weeks for books. They have to study on hallway floors and in stairwells, because there is no room. Several faculty have told me that whole chapters of their assigned reference works have been cut out of books by students who were desperate for the information. (With only three or four photocopying machines to service five thousand students, one can understand the level of frustration.)

I had an interesting conversation with a member of the law faculty about Irish culture and the Church. It is a recurrent theme everywhere, but one which only seems to elicit either pathological passion or total indifference whenever it is raised.

He is one of those unfortunate young men whose marriage is gone, and neither he nor his wife (they live apart, no kids) can do anything about it. There is no divorce in Ireland. He said there are thousands and thousands of relationships throughout the country that are marriages in name only, but the public myth of marital fidelity and bliss continues almost unabated here. In an otherwise idyllic and moral land, it is interesting to find this blend of irony, hypocrisy, and denial.

I crossed signals somehow and lost my ride home. Managed to make the walk in about forty-five minutes, however. Fortunately, it was a beautiful moonlit night.

Friday, March 29. Mary made hot cross buns this morning. Frankly, we couldn't remember the roots of the tradition or whether or not Good Friday was the day they were supposed to be eaten. Anyway, we decided we would each have one for breakfast, since it was a day of strict fast and abstinence. They were a "first" for Mary and the first I had eaten in more years than I could remember.

I checked the fuel oil level. Still had sixty gallons left. We probably should get some sort of award from a conservation committee.

We all went up to the Good Friday Tenebrae service in Castleconnell in the afternoon. Father Minogue is very "old school," of course, and he was constantly nudging and directing the flustered altar boys and instructing the congregation when to stand and when to sit.

The church was packed and the mix surprising, but I guess at Easter a lot of irregulars show up. Kate ran into a number of friends and that took the sting of solitude out of her religious experience.

Late in the afternoon, we went for a long bike ride through the back roads. At one point we came across a cowherd who was chasing an obviously recalcitrant cow. She refused to go with him, although all the rest of the herd was already lined up waiting to head in to the milking parlor.

I jokingly called over to the kid, "Is she giving you some trouble?"

"No," he said, "she's lost her calf and won't leave without it."

At that, the cow took off through the field, mooing, sniffing the ground, circling frantically. The boy was in hot pursuit with his collie right behind him. It was a real pastoral vignette. The cow disappeared behind a hedgerow and a few minutes later reappeared—with the calf. It was very poignant.

Saturday, March 30. Mary was racing around doing last minute chores for the holiday. As soon as the hour became respectable, I decided to wash the car and went over to Peter Rolls' next door to borrow a bucket. I poured some Mr. Proper (the Irish Mr. Clean) into a roasting pan and used a long handled floor broom, the head of which didn't fit in the pan. There is no outdoor spigot, and so I had to carry about ten buckets of water from the house and throw them at the car to rinse it off. I hoped no one was watching. It was a real Rube Goldberg operation. I also vacuumed, polished, and Windexed the interior. With a trained imagination, it looked like a new XJ6!

Kate and Charlene Bridgeman walked up to the 9:00 Mass that evening and Mary and I drove out to Glenstal Abbey.

The congregation gathered first in the Abbey Church and then moved outside. There was a huge bonfire. All the monks processed out in white robes. They chanted the "Lumine Christi" (Light of Christ). It was haunting, in the cool night with the fire crackling, listening to ancient Gregorian Chant against the stillness of the wooded Abbey. We all lit our candles, the first from the bonfire, then one from another, and returned to the church where the ceremony began.

The Mass was magnificently moving with alternating English and Latin prayers and Gregorian chant in both languages as well.

There were tea and "bickies" (cookies) in the refectory after Mass. I spotted Henry O'Shea and zeroed in on him because of something that had happened that evening. As I had sat down in the pew in church, there was about a half a seat available at the end. A showpiece in a swirling Inverness swept up the aisle and tried to get into the seat. Obviously he couldn't squeeze in, so he sat behind us. When I saw him at the reception, the Inverness was gone and he was wearing a tailor-made, three-piece, blue pinstripe suit with a watch chain the size of fence links. A bit outlandish. Henry said he was a religious offbeat who came from an old Galway family. He walked around calling all the monks "Domine." Seems he had tried to get into the Jesuits, but was turned down, had tried to get into Glenstal and was turned down. With his pedigree and money, I guess he ought to found his own "Order."

Sunday, March 31. Easter arrived with clouds and a fine mist. I had only slept about two and a half hours, so the day didn't look too promising. Mary's sister Jody was arriving for an overnight visit, and our neighbor Pat O'Sullivan had arranged "courtesy of the port" for her at Customs.

We got to the airport timely and I was ushered into Customs and then into the baggage area. When Jody arrived, she was quite stunned to see me there and even more so when they simply motioned us through. She had never received this treatment in hundreds of thousands of miles traveling all over the world. I felt great making her feel important.

For the rest of the day and into the evening, I was the proverbial fifth wheel. The three of them talked non-stop. Jody, the jet-setting designer/buyer sharing a million experiences with Mary and Kate, and the two of them regaling her with tales of Ireland. And, of course, there were endless discussions of the family.

Monday, April 1. It was a drab day, and I felt lousy, but the girls were perky as ever and simply picked up their conversations where they had left off sometime in the middle of the night.

We saw Jody off and came home. Mary plastered me with "Save the Baby Liniment," and I crashed.

Tuesday, April 2. I had another terrible night. Damned sinuses! I've never had this problem or been this sick in my life. Must have something to do with the climate here. I awoke early, but couldn't get back to sleep, so I decided to go in to school.

With the exception of a few hardy staff people, the place was deserted.

That night I had a bit of a blowout with Kate over her nonchalance and her failure to grasp a serious work ethic. She took it stoically (it was over house chores, general teenage slobbery, etc., nothing novel). I was overwrought by my performance and when I left the room, I burst into tears. I love that kid so much, and she is so good and so talented. It kills me to have to shock her with a little reality. Better now, I guess, but that doesn't make it any easier on Poppy.

Peter Rolls stopped by to inform us that Niamh had delivered a seven-pound, fifteen-ounce son and was doing well. He was headed back to the hospital but would be going out later. Would I join him? Of course.

About 10:00, there was a knock at the door. Tom Kinirons, our accountant neighbor from across the street was at the door.

"I have orders to deliver you to the Hurlers' Pub," he said.

I put on my coat and we left. Peter was rolling, but okay. We had a lot of neighborly laughs. Boys' night out. I've never really done that over the years. It was fun.

Wednesday, April 3. While getting dressed for school this morning, I looked out the window and saw the trash men coming down the road. Our stuff wasn't out because the huge jackdaws in the area peck away at the bags and then strew the contents all over the street and the yard. I let out a holler as the truck passed and disappeared. The next vision I saw was Mary and Kate piling huge garbage bags into the back seat of the car and tearing out of the driveway. They came back without the trash, and I didn't even ask whether the stuff made the truck or the ditch.

They have an interesting program for trash collection here. One can purchase a sticker for each bag at a variety of outlets for twenty-five pence. The stickers are then affixed to the bags. In our case, however, we never seem to have stickers, so Mary tapes the twenty-five pence coins to the bags. It is a matter of speculation how many of the coins find their way into the county coffers, although the moral level on such matters is generally pretty high here.

I spent most of the day writing.

Thursday, April 4. Winter returned with a fury this morning. It was raw, with cold rain, occasional hail and razor-sharp winds. (The natives refer to them as "thin" winds because of their blade-like effect.) I seriously considered not getting out of bed.

I drove in to school in all the "weather." The car now leaks in several places and it was not easy to dodge the drops. My hat blew off, the umbrella turned inside out, and my notes got soaked. Other than that, it was an uneventful trip.

Spent a few hours finishing up the first draft of my American Studies proposal, and in the midst of that, John Coakley stopped in and asked me if I would do a lecture for his Irish Politics class. I think I'll do something on American-Irish reaction to the situation in the North. It will not be what most people expect, though.

After dinner, Mary and I walked up to Finnegan's. To borrow a phrase from Fats Waller, "the joint was jumpin'."

The music stopped at about eleven (which is closing time), but slowly a few people began humming and singing a number of tunes. They seemed to blend in until, all of a sudden, two or three of us were at the center of a songfest. We did Ella Fitzgerald, show tunes, golden oldies, etc. It was "great craic (fun)," as they say in Ireland.

Friday, April 5. John Stapleton and Nick Rees both laid some lectures on me today for next term. With the commitments I already have to David Coombes in European Studies, Bernadette Whelan in History and Steve Dewar in the Business College, it should be a busy few months.

Saturday, April 6. Today was an absolutely ugly day—cold, pouring, and windy. It was one of the worst mornings I can remember since the hurricane last December. Rain and hail came down so hard and from so many directions in a swirling wind that it was impossible to see more than a few feet from the windows. The fields were covered with water. I wasn't going to stand in the rain or stand in a damp barn or sit in the car at Ashroe, so we scratched riding.

We all spent a cozy day reading, writing, and goofing off.

Sunday, April 7. If yesterday was ugly, today was "iffy." I was up before the roosters. The wind blew so hard last night it actually woke me up about 3:00. I thought the windows would come right through the draperies.

On the way in to Ryan's, I noticed the fishermen lining the shores. The water was so savage, though, that no one had ventured into the River.

Fr. Minogue celebrated the 11:00 Mass and delivered what was probably one of the three or four worst sermons in the history of Ireland. He rambled and raved, hemmed and hawed, and repeated himself at least a dozen times. It was like listening to Joyce's Ulysses, except Minogue wasn't going anywhere. He was awful and he spoke forever. I don't think he had anyone's attention when he finished. I'm surprised he didn't put himself to sleep! It's a shame, because that Mass attracts lots of teenagers and he completely turned them off.

Michael Laffan said to us outside, "All he ever talks about is sex and money—and it's negative, negative, negative."

That's a sure formula for blowing away a generation of kids.

We decided to go for a drive in the afternoon. At least the sun was out. Charlene Bridgeman and Kate put together a picnic lunch and off we went on the Dublin Road. About ten miles up, we turned east at Bird Hill and meandered aimlessly in the general direction of the Shannon, eventually reaching O'Brien's Bridge on the Clare side of the River. It's a neat little village at the widewaters of the river. There were quite a few water skiers out.

This was our first real venture into East Clare, so we stopped to check out the map. Then we wandered through several beautiful ridges in the Clare Hills and soon found ourselves in Cragganauwan, a prehistoric restoration project underwritten by philanthropist John Hunt. Hunt, incidentally, also donated the Hunt Museum located at the University, which houses a priceless collection of bronze, silver, gold and pottery artifacts, gemstones, and artworks. Similar to Loch Gur, Cragganauwan was the site of a Mesolithic community that actually built its houses on stilts in the middle of marshes and ponds—for protective purposes.

After several hours of prehistoric observation, Kate got off some very funny lines mocking her parents. As we passed one beautiful ancient tower, still in good shape but exposing about three layers of its walls, Mary expressed amazement at the construction and precision. Kate noted dryly, "Mom, we're talking major amusement here." I almost drove off the road.

I walked up to Finnegan's about ten o'clock and struck up a conversation with one of the regulars, Liam O'Shea. He talked about growing up in Ireland with a tyrannical church, with arrogant priests who ran villages like dictatorships. He told me how one priest had actually put his father's amusement hall out of business, even though it was little more than a gathering place. Said it was the sole income for his family of eleven. The priest had denounced the hall from the altar as a source of wickedness and depravity. The priest subsequently built one run by the Church (i.e., the priest) and made lots of money off it while Liam's family went broke. I could see why kids went into the religious life—if only to get a piece of the action. God, it must have been unbelievably corrupt in some towns. Unlike Russia, where the peasantry murdered the priests, here they just walked away and ignored them—and to a large degree still do.

Monday, April 8. It was tough getting Kate cranked up this morning—back-to-school blues, etc. The bus never showed up, so I drove her in. We were a few minutes late, but she went in with a crowd, so I guess everything was okay.

I spent some time later in the morning with Tom Lynes from the British Labour Party. I'd met him in Cork last fall. Since we were both political "operatives" rather than elected politicians, we had a great deal in common and shared lots of gossip about British and American politics. Their parliamentary system, with its rigid party control and partisan discipline is a far cry from the free wheeling "frontier" politics played in the States. I have great respect for the notion of party loyalty, but there is such a wide streak of maverick in most Americans, both politicians and lay people, I doubt that a parliamentary design could even function in the U.S.

Mary had to go in to town for a meeting after dinner, so Kate and I spent the evening together. It turned out to be rather momentous. I'm not sure what triggered me, but I proceeded to spill my guts to her about where we are, where we were, and where we are likely to be. I didn't want to overload her circuits, but she said how thankful she was that I had finally taken her into my confidence. She didn't really have much of a handle on our presence in Limerick. It was a very frank discussion about money, responsibility, love, sacrifice, real values, education, friendships. I think it was the closest I felt to her since I used to hold her little body in my forearms.

Mary was quite miffed that I had had the conversation without her presence and input.

Tuesday, April 9. It was pretty cold this morning, both outdoors and in the house! I told Mary I'd make coffee for her, then proceeded to start writing in the kitchen and forgot the coffee completely. The cold in the house had by then turned to ice. Mary wasn't just upset with me, however. She feels physically unwell, emotionally strung-out, homesick, professionally frustrated, and concerned that we still don't know where my program at the University is going.

Wednesday, April 10. Paddy Tyrell arrived for dinner about 7:30. We had tea and then a magnificent lasagna dinner, the best Mary ever made. The dinner conversation was lively and discursive.

We touched on everything—politics, society, families, the Church, linguistics. It was important for Kate to see someone other than her father engage in intellectual sport.

Contrary to a lot of popular sentiment, Paddy gave a vigorous first-hand defense of the Irish Christian Brothers and their educational program. I have heard many people contend that the Order was replete with sadists and misfits. He admitted there were a few psychos over the years, but said the same was true in the public schools in England at the time. Much of his defense was financial. The Brothers had saved the government a fortune and brought an education to the peasantry. It was the salvation of the country and the breeding ground for independence, unlike the Latin American countries where the peasantry remained (remains) largely uneducated and illiterate. He made an interesting point about the Jesuits missing the boat—all the more interesting because he is one. The Jesuits, he said, taught primarily the rich and the powerful in a sort of educational trickle-down philosophy.

Thursday, April 11. In what appeared to be a gesture of independence, Kate announced this morning that she didn't need anyone to get her breakfast or lunch today. I noticed when I came down that her lunch was not made and that there were no dirty breakfast dishes. Upon enquiry, she said she'd had a hot cross bun and some orange juice, but the juice hadn't even been out of the fridge yet. She had lied. Not a whopper, but it was a first. I poured milk into a bowl of corn flakes and said, "Eat!" She ate.

I went over to Nabil Adawy's office to chat about the International Relations program. He was not concerned about Ed Walsh's question over self-financing. Said the research end of the Masters would generate about seventy thousand pounds, enough to pay himself and another lecturer. I didn't say anything but silently calculated that this figure would leave me in the throes of poverty. I had already forsaken an income for the entire school year and didn't see how I could survive.

There was another fly in the ointment, of course, which caused me considerable concern. The Department head was opposed to the program—at least for the time being—and that posed a significant impediment. It simply wouldn't fly without his support.

After dinner, the family went up to Castleconnell Church for Confirmation rehearsal.

(In Ireland, a parish is considered as a geographical area rather than as a neighborhood church. In fact, most parishes have several churches within them. While we go to Mass at Ahane, Ahane is but one of the three churches in the Parish of Castleconnell. Since Castleconnell Church is the principal church in the Parish of Castleconnell, it is the venue for Confirmation.)

The rehearsal was right out of the nineteenth century. "We'll practice kneeling down, now. We'll practice saying the Our Father, now."

Incredible. Fr. Minogue addressing the entire congregation, children and adults alike, as so many five-year-olds. He went on about cameras in church and about dinners and parties after the ceremony. The first were banned because they were "unsacred" and the second were discouraged because they were frivolous—along with gifts and money. Michael Laffan's words came back to me: "All he ever talks about is sex and money." Tonight it was money.

66

The candidates and their sponsors (Kate had asked Madeline Bridgeman to be hers) were marched, a row at a time, up to the altar where Fr. Minogue tapped each kid on the head and then ordered all to return to their pews. The entire class of sixty-eight kids and sixty-eight sponsors went through this drill. I didn't know whether to laugh or cry.

Friday, April 12. It was a miserably cold and gloomy day. We all took a hand at cleaning up the house for tomorrow's onslaught of relatives, and Mary was up until the wee hours preparing for the Confirmation party. (She obviously hadn't listened very attentively to Fr. Minogue's stern lecture Friday.)

Saturday, April 13. I had a lot of work to do this morning, building fires, moving furniture, vacuuming, polishing, and driving over to Glenstal Abbey to pick up cousin Phillip Ryan. Mary was moving like a house afire and Kate had gone across the street to get her hair plaited.

We left a few minutes early for Castleconnell Church and grabbed two front row seats in the balcony of the "wing." It was a beautiful but simple ceremony. The Confirmation was half as rigid as the practice. The Bishop was very gracious with the kids. We watched with pride as he confirmed Kate. By now, she was almost bursting with joy and had a beatific smile. I did get a little wistful, though. This was the first major event in our married life at which Fr. Jack Morse had not been a participant.

After Mass, we stopped to chat with the Bishop ("Your grace"). Father Minogue, in his welcoming remarks, had actually called him "My Lord Bishop." I nearly fell out of the balcony.

I was taken aback when the Bishop said he knew I was teaching at the University. There are no secrets in Ireland.

The whole clan returned to "Lauran" and we had a wonderful afternoon. Bridget Hehir regaled us with tales of Delia (Mary's Grandmother) and what it was like to grow up in Bouloughera. She said Delia not only had to walk the three miles each way to school every day, but had to ford the River Fleuer as well. Bridget mentioned that they have only had electricity out there for twenty-seven years and paved roads only since 1957. Until then they had to walk across the fields carrying sacks of foodstuffs home. Couldn't even drive a wagon in the bogs. They used an ass to ferry the goods across the creeks and rivers. Very primitive, but very recent as well.

Sunday, April 14. We got up at the crack of dawn to drive out to Shannon Airport. My old pal from Washington, Mike Flaherty, and his wife Evalene, were flying back to the States this morning. They had been over in Kerry for a few days, but we hadn't been able to get together and wanted at least to have a cup of coffee with them. They were the first familiar Washington faces we had seen in eight months.

When we got home, I found a cow in Peter Rolls' driveway and ran over to warn him. His little ones frequently wander around outdoors in the morning, and a scared cow might do almost anything. As it turned out, the cow had already been on the rampage. She'd destroyed Carey's and O'Sullivan's flower gardens. There is a certain down-to-earth atmosphere in our neighborhood.

Monday, April 15. Traditionally in Ireland, Confirmed students get the day off, but not at Protestant schools. Villiers is nominally Church of Ireland, so Kate had to return to class this morning.

It was a beautiful day. The gorse and blackthorn are all in bloom. So, unfortunately, is my lawn—about a foot high. I have a power mower, with petrol in it, but I literally don't know how to get the damn thing started!

This is Rag Week at the University. It's an old Irish tradition of springtime goofing off, drinking, sunning, and raising money for charities through controlled zaniness (kids tossed in the pool, etc.).

There were football, hurling, and soccer matches all over the place. The courtyard of the Stables was full of pint-drinkers, and lovers were sprawled out on the grass. It could have been any college in the world on a spring day.

Tuesday, April 16. John Stapleton stopped me in the hall to discuss the International Relations program. He knows Henry Ellis is currently opposed to it, not in principle, but because of priorities. John is personally very supportive and wants me not only to stay at the University but to develop a full-scale American Studies curriculum as well. I leveled with him, though. I told him I had made a moral commitment to see my lecture schedule through until June, even without a salary, but I couldn't afford to stay beyond that point. He understood completely.

Wednesday, April 17. We had a minor crisis on the home front. Mary had left the water heater for the sinks on all night. We have an electric switch that heats sinks and showers in seconds. It is designed as a money-saver and an element of energy conservation. It is tremendously effective, but only if it is shut off immediately after being used. The system is so intense, however, it costs a fortune if left on. Electricity is inordinately expensive in Ireland, anyway. I think there are only three generating plants in the entire country. Seems strange in a place surrounded by tidal waters.

I had a rather quiet day in the office, although I did accomplish some work on a bibliography and I managed to get some reading done.

There was a lot of action elsewhere on the campus, though. The students were very busy kidnapping secretaries as part of Rag Week, and then holding them for ransom over in the Stables. The more civilized supervisors didn't bother to ransom the girls until late in the afternoon and in fact many of them offered themselves as joint 'hostages' in the bar. The less understanding ransomed them early on, much to the regret of the secretaries.

Thursday, April 18. I met with John O'Brien this morning. He is the Deputy Headmaster at the Crescent Comprehensive school in Limerick. Crescent, while technically a part of the National (public) School System, is still very much a Jesuit School. It has a reputation for excellent academic discipline, good sports, and splendid extracurricular activities.

We arrived too late last fall to enroll Kate, so we decided to make an early application this time around.

John is a very impressive man. Tall and spare with white hair and rimmed glasses, he looks like a middle-aged Barry Fitzgerald. He speaks with a pronounced but "educated" Cork accent. "Street" Corkese is unfathomable.

He explained that Crescent goes out of its way to accommodate other "institutions," e.g., the University, so I had to imply at least that we were going to be around for quite some time. The competition for admission is bloody awful. The school is highly unionized and by contract they cannot have more than twenty-eight kids in each class. This puts enormous pressure on the Admissions Office. The politics of it are fierce.

I came away with no commitment, but I had managed to get one foot and one toe in the door.

Back at school, I finally worked out my lecture schedule in Public Administration, European Integration, International Relations (undergraduate), Politics, History Seminar, and Business. It is a fairly heavy schedule for the rest of the term. By comparison to most of my colleagues, it is a light classroom load, but because I have started each of my courses from scratch, I find myself spending about ten hours in research and writing for every 1 hour in the classroom. In theory, of course, the burden will be eased as I progress from year to year. We'll see.

The view from my office was very special today. The foliage is coming out, there are hundreds of red azaleas beneath my windows, and the hills beyond the Shannon are awash in blossoming white blackthorns, pink cherry trees, and fulsome yellow gorse.

Mary drove in to pick me up. There had been a bad shimmy in the car, so she had the front tire changed. The shimmy is gone, but the tire isn't very good. The car will probably get us to a garage in a pinch, though. (As one of my neighbors says, "It'll get ye from A to B.") Meanwhile, the chrome strip on the driver's side has come unscrewed and a new leak has developed in the windshield. With the driver's door still partially unhinged and the front passenger seat unhitched from the floor, the car is a hoot to ride in!

Friday, April 19. I spent most of the day mowing our foot-high lawn (after Pat O'Sullivan got the machine started for me). Mary was at the University for a Women's Studies seminar.

After we finished the dinner dishes, Kate invited some of her girlfriends over, and Mary and I went out to a pub called "O'Shea's." We had heard about it from Patti Punch. It's on the Old Cork Road, about ten minutes from the house over the back roads. If we hadn't been looking for it, we'd have missed it. It consisted of a couple of old run-together cement cottages painted pastel orange, with a small Guinness sign outside. It wasn't six feet from the roadway. We pulled off the road and literally couldn't find the entrance. I spotted a door, a simple door with nothing written on it. I didn't know if I was walking into a milking parlor, somebody's kitchen, or what.

As I opened the door, I saw a small semi-horseshoe bar with an elderly woman behind it and four guys sitting there whispering among themselves. I had that sinking feeling I experienced the first time I ventured into the bar in the Black Swan: they are mentally dissecting me. What am I doing disturbing their little nest? Unlike the Black Swan, however, here everyone smiled and nodded and we were obviously welcome.

As unprepossessing as the place was, we learned that it is a regular stop for many of the University faculty and administration. It was a fun departure from our routine.

Saturday, April 20. It rained overnight, so I was pleased and proud that I had finished the lawn. Mary and Kate went off to Ashroe, and I wrote. When they returned, I built a great fire in the den, and replenished the coal three times. It was toasty. Mary said it was the warmest she'd felt since we left America. Kate seems to have adapted to the weather. Mary and I are cold constantly.

All in all, it was a fantastic day, topped off with a gorgeous pot roast and, later, several readings from Robert Frost.

Sunday, April 21. It was a slow day for all of us, but warmed up after Mass in the evening. I think every kid in County Limerick made at least a cameo appearance at our house. There were tapes running at about eight decibels in both Kate's room and the living room, with six or seven dance routines all going at once in various parts of the house.

The phone rang perhaps twenty times, the doorbell, at least as often. There were bodies in and out. It was like Dagwood's house. I took my leave after about an hour and a half and went for a long, long walk up the Murroe Road.

The kids all love our house. They know Mary and I are a little zany and a lot of fun. We are also the only household for miles around large enough to accommodate a mob scene and crazy enough to put up with one.

Monday, April 22. On my way in to school I saw scattered clouds moving almost due south. I noticed them because it was so unusual. The wind is generally west to east off the Atlantic in this part of Ireland.

I had a laughable experience. The Dublin Institute was supposed to reimburse me for my travel and meals when I went up to lecture. The check had never arrived. Mary O'Brien in our office called to find out what was going on, and was told, verbatim, "The check is in the post (mail)." It was so innocent, it was too funny to satirize. I might never get the check, but I did get a good chuckle.

Tuesday, April 23. The power at the University actually went off this afternoon. The ESB, the semi-state electricity board, went on strike and shut down all the power plants. Talk about a banana republic!

I made the airline reservations for June 28 today. Finding the money for the tickets, the cargo and a bunch of current household bills is going to be a real treat. The first things I'll pay for are the tickets. At least we can get home.

I remain very frustrated and very broke. So far this little venture has cost me over fifty thousand dollars in cash and several times that in lost income. We still have places to visit and visitors to host, so there will be additional expenditures over the next two months. My gut instinct is simply to borrow more money and say, "to hell with it."

Wednesday, April 24. I planned to accomplish a number of things at school today, but the power kept going on and off. If the strikers and management seemed close to an agreement, the lights came back on. If someone got ticked off, the lights went out. I was convinced Peter Sellers was handling the negotiations!

Henry Ellis was pessimistic about the American Studies initiative when we talked this morning. I have been urged by a number of colleagues to go directly to the President to press my case. Between financial stress and academic uncertainty, my level of frustration is becoming alpine.

Thursday, April 25. I spent a good portion of today drumming up support for American studies. I am still trying to get the Foundation interested in tapping some of their membership, since frankly, I think such a curriculum would induce further contributions to the school from well-heeled Irish Americans.

In a meeting with John Coakley, he agreed to participate in the program. He is so insightful, so street smart, so bright, and so dedicated, he would make a tremendous contribution—if I can get it off the ground. John Stapleton, in his deliciously articulate manner, described Coakley, the Mayo man, as a "classic West of Ireland anarchist." How apt.

Friday, April 26. Kate was leaving on a weekend class trip to the wastelands of the Burren in County Clare today. It was an archaeological outing. Theoretically, everything was packed last night before she went to bed. This morning, however, there was panic and ambivalence. Deep down, I know she was a little afraid of the trip, but it didn't come out that way. Everything else but. She didn't feel good. She didn't feel right not wearing her uniform to school (even though they had been given permission to come to school ready to travel). She wanted to go home.

"Pop, you just don't understand," she said. "I want a ride to school. I want to take the bus. Mom, will you bring my things in later? I don't need a hat. Will you drive me to the bus?"

I was dizzy at that point.

I drove her to the bus stop and she didn't want to get out. Then the tears came.

"Okay, I'll drive you to school, Button."

We got to the school parking lot.

"I can't get out—not in my jeans!"

Right about then I think St. Francis himself would have given her a kick in the tail. To top it off, four boys in her class showed up—in uniform. She almost died. I said the only way we find out the "drill" is by asking the boys. Reluctantly, she called them. They came over and said the Headmaster had released everyone except the boy boarders. She got out, all smiles—the fulfillment of peer approval, no doubt. At that juncture, she barely acknowledged my presence. I gave her a quick peck and left. I had served my purpose. It was probably the first time in her life that she had been confronted with the possibility of being non-de-rigueur.

I laughed to myself all the way home. I thought, "If only she knew how we were both fumbling at the same time, and how her adolescence was as much of a learning experience for me as it was for her. . ."

After a day of research and writing, I met Mary at the Stables.

We were joined by some friends from New York who had just arrived with neon signs. Up to that point I hadn't realized how we had come to blend in with the scenery and how much Americans stand out in a crowd of Irishmen. The contrast was very sharp.

Americans dress well, exude an air of confidence, and tend to be demonstrative. Without meaning to offend or intimidate, they simply come across as cocky and uninhibited.

We did the campus tour and then I made reservations for dinner at 8:30. The late daylight threw us off schedule, and we didn't arrive at the restaurant until 9:20. It was beginning to get dusky.

One of our guests asked, "Will they hold reservations this long?"

I said, "You're in Ireland. Not to worry."

The place was packed, but there was our table—waiting for us. Our waitress acted as though we were right on target, which, by Irish standards, we were.

Saturday, April 27. It was a cold and miserable day and with Kate away, a perfect day to loaf before the fire. I managed to get all the bills paid. Another month, another miracle!

Martha Laffan came by for dinner and we sat in front of the hearth. I mentioned a funny line Kate had got off the other day. She and her friends were discussing an upcoming show on television that night and they asked her if she planned to watch it. (Of course, by design we still don't have a TV.)

Kate said, "No, we only get one channel on our set, Bord na Mona."

Bord na Mona, of course, is the government's cut-turf monopoly. Martha doubled up laughing.

Sunday, April 28. It was still cold and windy when we walked up to Mass. I don't know what has happened to spring.

Kate arrived home bubbling over. I have no idea what they acquired in archaeological lore, but apparently the weekend was a smashing social success.

After a long walk in the evening, I stopped in at Finnegan's. A number of GAA members from the Ahane Club were there for a post-match gathering, and I struck up a conversation about the structure and management of the Association. The president of the local club told me the national organization is "getting liberal." I couldn't wait to hear where and how.

"They now accept advertising," he said.

Nothing about women or girl participants (who are still banned) or transathletics such as soccer, rugby, and other "alien" games (which are forbidden on GAA fields), of course. But they are "getting liberal." 'Tis in the eye of the beholder!

Monday, April 29. Today was my day in the box with the Business students. I had coffee with one of the faculty beforehand and we had an interesting conversation on the impact of taxation on capital formation in Ireland. He said most of the middle class in the country are being murdered by income taxes. The current rate is about fifty-three percent on everything over eleven thousand pounds. On a floating scale, eleven thousand pounds would be fifteen to twenty thousand dollars—a very oppressive level.

The lecture went exceptionally well. I spoke for one hour and then entertained questions for an additional hour. And subsequently did a follow-up hour and a half impromptu Q & A at the University Club. Three and a half hours in front of one hundred and fifty students is a draining experience.

During the program, I addressed the U.S. political system, the structure of the Federal Government, the points of vulnerability in the legislative process, and the role of the business community in the formulation of foreign policy, particularly as it relates to trade and commerce. The questions ranged all over the lot—corruption in Washington, the future of GATT, the soundness of the U.S. economy, the role of lobbyists, etc. It was most engaging.

Tuesday, April 30. I made arrangements today to participate in John Coakley's "Northern Ireland" series next month. That gives me adequate time to meet with Prof. Paul Arthur at the University of Ulster and Prof. Con O'Leary at Queen's University in Belfast. They are both specialists in conflict resolution and both very knowledgeable about the politics and sociology of Northern Ireland. I need that dimension. I also need more current information from friends in Washington in order to pull the lecture together. It's billed as an "American Perspective on the Situation in the North."

I ran into Kate's German teacher at school. She teaches part-time at the University as well. When she wished me "Happy Birthday" I asked how she knew and she said Kate told her she had to do a birthday party for me and so her homework wouldn't be ready this morning. Bells and whistles went off. She'd fibbed again. I called the house and told Kate I had run into Mrs. Kearney. She immediately owned up. And cried. I told her Mrs. Kearney was disappointed that her work was slipping. Then it all blurted out. "I'm only taking German because Mom said it would please you!" This kid already has an MA in BS. Lots of chatter at dinner. Kate was very witty and sardonic.

She said, "All Pop wants to talk about is what I'll be doing in Law School. All Mom wants to talk about is what I did when I was three. Can't anybody talk about today?"

So I talked about "today" and today's homework, and she didn't like that.

I went up to Finnegan's late in the evening and one of my farmer-neighbors grabbed me. He really wanted to talk. As we sat there, he unfolded his whole domestic story and I realized that I had "arrived." Here was a local farmer, albeit well educated and sophisticated, who wanted to talk about the real Irish world with an outsider. Before I knew it, he had led me through his own broken marriage, a wife who had walked out with a third party, the tragedy of single parentage of three kids, and the frustration (and gossip) of attempted companionship. Because of the ban on divorce, this fellow in his thirties is stranded.

He's a chap of great integrity. The oldest of his family, he was left the man of the house when his father died young. He'd like to emigrate, mainly I think for social and marital reasons, but the cost of transporting and financing a family of four is too heavy at this point. So, like thousands of others, he's stuck here. It was a fascinating monologue. (I just listened.)

Wednesday, May 1. It was a perfectly beautiful spring day. If I were a "nine-to-fiver," this would definitely have been a sick leave day.

When I got home from school, Mary and Kate had prepared a traditional birthday dinner. Good china, candles, steak, mushrooms, rice, salad, and my mother-in-law's chocolate cake.

I had heard some rather depressing news during the day, so I wandered up to Finnegan's to get the details. Young Tommy Hassett, son of the fellow who was helping me with the O'Gorman genealogy in County Clare, and uncle of one of Kate's closest girlfriends at Villiers was killed in a freak moped accident. He was only thirty-two. It seems his bike hit the curb, he flew over the handlebars and his helmet wasn't on securely. He was severely brain damaged and they took him off life support.

My conversation-mate from last night came in and we were soon knee-deep in chatter again. We got into sports and before long, the GAA and the Church worked their way into the conversation. He said up till a few years ago, there wasn't a GAA club in the country that did not have a priest as president, coach, trainer or treasurer. It was automatic when a priest was assigned to a parish. In the rural areas, the loop was closed securely by the involvement of the Fianna Fail cumann (local committee). It is small wonder that only about 20% of the people in the country still go to church regularly.

Thursday, May 2. I called Paul Arthur in Belfast to see if we could get together to discuss the Northern Irish political scene. When he answered the phone, frankly I wasn't sure he'd remember me. He is a prominent academician, political commentator, lecturer, author, etc. He is very highly respected in Irish political and intellectual circles.

His response was immediate and effusive. Of course he remembered me and would love to get together. He invited me to stay with him and his family while I'm in the North.

Mary Hassett came over to have dinner with Kate tonight. Her whole family is naturally devastated, over the tragic loss of her uncle.

Friday, May 3. I spent the entire morning writing and, at lunchtime, Mary joined me at the Student Center. Michael D. Higgins, a Labor Party T.D.(Taichtde Dail), a Member of the Irish Parliament, Mayor of Galway, Professor of Politics at University College, Galway, and a very accomplished poet, had a scheduled reading. It was powerful. The collection is called "The Betrayal." In keeping with typical Irish efficiency, there were no copies of the book available for sale. He read from the one volume, and from some unpublished papers as well. There were rich tones, metaphors, powerful imagery, and synecdoche. I winced, cried, roared with laughter, and just plain hung on as he discoursed his way through Irish politics, the Irish country culture, world liberation philosophy, family emotions, and memories.

I had a long talk with him afterward. I said I felt as though I had been sitting through Dylan Thomas. He beamed. Thomas was a hero. Somehow I knew that. I cited similar lines in Thomas' works and his, and we both laughed at the borderline plagiarism. Thomas was every student's hero in the Fifties when Higgins and I were growing up.

I called Paul Arthur in the afternoon to beg off my Monday trip. Gerry Warren, who had been Dick Nixon's Press Secretary, is doing a guest lecture that day and I want to see him. Paul was very understanding. We rescheduled for May 15.

We made plans to go to the Hassett wake up in Newport. Kate said the funeral began about half-seven (7:30). I said no. The wake was tonight; the funeral would be tomorrow. We enquired among the neighbors about calling hours. There usually aren't any, in the structured American sense. Most people simply drop in—at 8:30, or 10:00, or midnight. Someone even suggested a midnight Rosary was not all that uncommon. Anyway, we left for Newport a little after eight o'clock. It's about a twenty-minute drive.

In a town with two crossroads and one side street, we couldn't find Meehan's funeral home—even after three enquiries. When we finally pinpointed the place (there were no signs), a woman indicated we had missed the "funeral." It had left for Ahane Church at 8:15. We'd passed the church on the way to Newport and noticed cars parked as much as a half-mile away. I thought it was a wedding, another funeral, or perhaps a First Friday Mass. In fact the Hassett mourners were already there for the 'return.' In Ireland, a "funeral" is the procession that returns the body from the home or funeral parlor to the church. The mourners then follow and when they get to the church, the Rosary is said. The Funeral Mass doesn't take place until the next day. Kate had been right.

The church was bulging and flowing out into the yard and the street by the time we arrived. It was the largest gathering I had seen anywhere in Ireland. The old people—raw-boned red farmers with their plain, crease-ridden wives, friends of the parents, and young people, friends of the dead man and his twenty-nine-year-old widow and three kids. The crowd all muttered Hail Mary's to themselves in the churchyard, staring at the ground or into the rustling trees. Very somber, but with no tears. The Irish do not cry much. They wear worry right out on their sleeves, but it is usually mute. Centuries of poverty, oppression, and hardship have taught them how useless it is to show emotion.

Dropping Mary and Kate back at the house, I walked on up to Finnegan's. There were scores of people there who had come directly from the church. Most of the conversation centered naturally enough on the accident.

I ran into my neighbor, Alan O'Reilly, and asked him about the casket in church. He said the casket would "lie in state," if you will, overnight. And then he floored me. He said even if there were a wedding scheduled before the Funeral Mass, the casket would stand there in the front of the church and the couple would be married next to it!

The oldest Hassett girl (six) is scheduled to make her First Communion tomorrow. The Funeral Mass is planned for 1:00 in the afternoon. This means that the casket will be sitting there for her and the family during "her" ceremony. Seems a bit gruesome. Life, death, marriage, family. They all go on uninterrupted in a society still close to the earth.

As Alan and I talked, I noticed Tom Berkery in his tweed cap and his tweed jacket sitting at the end of the bar. He had obviously been there a while. I asked if the pension checks had come out this week.

"Yes. Today."

We both laughed out loud.

Saturday, May 4. It was a very cold and windy morning when we left for Ashroe. By the time we got up there, it was Siberian. Since they had planned an outdoor dressage, it meant that yours truly had to stand out in the wind.

Kate rode Isabel, and she was excellent. Perfect posture, in total control of the horse. She was a young lady very sure of herself, so unlike the little girl I had brought up here eight months ago. She trotted, cornered, cantered, and jumped to perfection. Her timing was great as well. She guided Isabel over the traces like a pro. I nearly burst.

Ashroe is beautiful now. The setting is magnificent anyway, nestled in the lush rolling foothills of Tipperary. The fields are covered with daisies, violets, and rhododendron, and there is an infinite variety and color of flowers climbing the centuries-old stone walls. The perfumed heath is in full bloom.

We went in to the University to the Irish National Self Portrait Gallery where several additions were being unveiled this afternoon. The fact that each of the artists was there in the flesh made the event all the more exciting.

John and Margaret Stapleton stopped by the house afterward, and they verbally took us back through the early history of the University. They filled in a lot of the blanks for us on President Walsh, Professor Mulcahy, and Jack Daly, the Chairman of the Board.

I had misinterpreted Daly's role here. He impressed me as a corporate type who had made a pile of money and took over the Shannon Development Corporation, whence came his springboard to the University. He smoked big cigars, strutted, always wore three-piece pinstripe suits, and appeared a bit pompous.

Today, however, as we were about to go in the Jean Monet Theater for the portrait unveilings, I had spotted him in a sport coat and slacks. He had recognized me and stuck out his hand. As we walked along, I had mentioned my Fianna Fail connections (I'd heard that he had Fianna Fail roots.)

He had wheeled around and said, "I'm Fianna Fail. How the hell do you think I got all these chairmanships?"

That blew my mind. I had totally misread the guy. A former Chairman of the Clare County Council, and a committed Fianna Fail activist, he was a "pol" from head to foot. The politics of this place and the pervasive influence of the government in academia have taken on a new meaning for me.

Sunday, May 5. After Mass at Ahane, I dove into the newspapers. Mary and Kate left on a long bike ride through the country. The foliage is beautiful now, even though many of the fruit blossoms (cherries, sloes, apples, and blackberries) have gone green. Our little road is lush.

Kate took a nasty spill off her bike, which required a dressing and a splint for her arm—both supplied by Anne Gunthrop, a nurse-neighbor.

I stopped up at Finnegan's late in the evening and had a chat with Eamon Lawler, the Fianna Fail chairman for Ahane. We talked about Jack Daly and his appointments to all the boards.

"Of course," Eamon said knowingly, "they go with the job (of Fianna Fail activist)."

The government has its hands deep into everything in this country.

I wasn't at Finnegans for very long, but a few things happened that bespeak my acceptance in the community. One fellow asked me if I'd enjoy digging turf some day with him. A few minutes later another invited me to go rabbit hunting with him.

And then a third guy approached me and said, "I see you going to Communion every Sunday."

My God, do they have Communion police here? In any event, it's a comfortable feeling to know that they've invited me behind the hedgerows of their culture.

Monday, May 6. Kate was up and gone early this morning. She obviously couldn't wait to show off the sling, hopefully elicit some sympathy, and suffer in public.

Mary dropped me off at school for Gerry Warren's lecture. Nixon's former press officer, he's now Editor of the San Diego Union and a regular on the MacNeil-Lehrer News Hour.

Gerry was very direct in his comments to the students—although most of his remarks went over their politically unsophisticated heads. They are young and don't know much about U.S. political history. Watergate is a part of the political lexicon worldwide, but it has no flesh for seventeen or eighteen-year-old Irish students. Anyway, he was enjoyable. We shared a laugh over the silliness of breaking into Spencer Oliver's office (Democratic Headquarters at the Watergate building).

The most dramatic moment in his remarks was the point at which he said:

"I had intended to talk about post-Gulf politics, but with the medical bulletin out of Bethesda Hospital, obviously I want to discuss that with you."

74

I nearly fell over. I had bought the *Irish Times* and the *London Times* blindly a few minutes before, but never even looked at the headlines.

Bush was in the hospital with an arrhythmic heart; no one knew how serious it was, and Quayle was poised to take over. The prospects were almost terrifying. Warren was painfully distressed about Quayle, but confined himself to the fact that he had not had life experiences like World War II. He didn't call him a flaming idiot, but he was not all that laudatory.

I took the bus into town to pick up our airline tickets, only to learn that the Aer Lingus operator had given me the wrong address. It was about ten blocks off—and they had moved to the new office a year ago. Chalk up another one for Irish efficiency.

There was a bit of hoopla on the way home from school at night. The Dublin Road was jammed with cars—more than usual—at the roundabout (traffic circle). The County Council has proposed turning the land on the circle into a "halting site" for the Travelers, and many of the local residents were out with placards protesting the move.

I guess I sympathize with the free style of the Travelers (Tinkers or Itinerants as they are often called) but, within a week, they would turn the entire area into one huge trashcan. They are unmercifully sloppy, with garbage, scrap iron, dogs, and kids all over the streets. I wish I understood more about them. They have some mystical hold on the politicians. No one will touch them. Most of their kids go around filthy dirty and half-naked, even in the dead of winter. Many of the kids are obviously undernourished (I personally saw it in their eyes when they were camped at the end of our road), and yet a substantial number of the Travelers are well off, driving forty-five thousand dollar vans and cars. Hundreds, maybe thousands of them own beautiful homes in Rathkeale in Southwest Co. Limerick. In any other society, the parents would be charged with child abuse and cited for all sorts of public nuisance and public health violations. For some reason I have not yet fathomed, the authorities here simply look the other way.

The history of the Travelers is almost as murky as the current political approach to their behavior. Some scholars believe their roots go back to several centuries B.C., while others trace them to the upheavals of the sixteenth and seventeenth centuries when thousands of Irish were thrown off their own land. Wherever and whenever they first surfaced, today they are numerically insubstantial, probably less than one percent of the population.

The derivation of "Traveller" or "Itinerant" is fairly straightforward, but it took me a while to divine the name "Tinker."

In Irish, a ceard is a smith(y) and a tinceard is obviously a tinsmith, which, at one time, was a principal trade of these people.

As nearly as I can figure out, they are not ethnically related to Romany Gypsies, who have been traveling the globe for centuries as well.

It was a quiet evening, except for the arrival on the doorstep of a stray female Jack Russell. Adorable puppy. We tried all around to find the owner but to no avail. Dogs come and go almost daily in this neighborhood.

It was comical to watch Kate. Although she could barely do anything for herself all day, and reveled in the attention her injury brought, somehow she managed to muster enough strength and organization to fold blankets for the dog, pick the dog up, lay out a rug for her, feed her, etc. (The healing powers of a puppy are amazing.)

By bedtime, both Kate and the dog were ensconced on her bed fast asleep. Mary had forbidden Kate to put the dog IN bed. Kate put the dog ON the bed, but completely covered. She'll make a great lawyer!

Tuesday, May 7. I spent some time this morning on the computer identifying possible reference works for my History Seminar lecture. The latest thing in the library was published in 1974! Fortunately, I already have a lot of statistical information and anecdotal details and I have fashioned a pretty good historical perspective. My plan is to discuss the rise, development, and metamorphosis of political parties in the United States. It could be considered as an entire course, but I will try to synthesize it into one and a half hours. I've already done a broad mental outline, and today I put together the sketches of a physical outline. I want this to be a scholarly piece, in keeping with the norms of the series.

The dog is still with us. She's already acquired a name, "Shadow," and, of course, everyone believes she responds to that name now. The dumb dog doesn't even know where it is, but it recognizes it's new name immediately! The power of imagination is overwhelming.

Wednesday, May 8. As I was having coffee this morning, I realized that the cattle have been missing from our back fields for a few days. I suppose they have been taken up to the abattoir in Nenagh, in County Tipperary. They were about the fourth herd we've seen since our arrival. I don't know how long they are grazed before slaughter, but it can't be more than five or six weeks. Anyway, there will probably be a new herd (six to eight head) within a few days. These small herds are the underpinning of a lively cattle industry in Ireland that feeds much of the European Community and the Middle East. Even in the remoteness of an island six hundred miles from the Arctic Circle, we are still part of the global economy.

I got roped into an evening concert of sorts at Crescent School. It was two and a half hours of sheer agony. The orchestra couldn't have found the right notes with a road map, and the string section sounded like the cats were still attached.

I said to John O'Brien on my way out, "Tonight was in lieu of purgatory."

He understood completely.

Thursday, May 9. Today was Ascension Thursday. Mary and Kate gobbled up a quick breakfast and flew off to the 8:00 Mass at the Salesian Church and then in to Villiers. I wrote all morning, and when Mary returned, headed in to a later Mass.

I had a return call from Archbishop Cassidy of Tuam in County Galway. It was in regard to a request from an old friend of mine in the States, Edna Kelly, who had been a Congresswoman from Brooklyn for twenty years. It seems her uncle had been Cassidy's predecessor once or twice removed, and she was interested in getting a picture of him. I said I would see what I could do to facilitate the matter and gave the Bishop's office a ring. Little did I realize that he would respond personally.

Before I returned his call, I thought I would check on the correct way to address him, the proper ecclesiastical protocol, if you will. (Fr. Minogue's outrageous "My Lord Bishop" kept racing through my mind.) I asked the secretaries in the office (who else?). We got to howling, "Your Lordship, Your Worship, Your Grace." Mary O'Brien finally found someone who knew, and we settled on "M'lord" and laughed irreverently.

Friday, May 10. It was another beautiful morning with little pink and white puffy clouds drifting in off the ocean.

While I was writing, the Archbishop's office called. They are searching the archives. If no loose picture turns up, they'll let me come up there and shoot one from their "rogue's gallery." It's about an hour and a half drive in normal traffic.

Mary picked me up and we walked over to the Stables. The place was packed. It was the University Societies Dinner night at the Limerick Inn. The Stables was apparently the "staging area."

What an array! All those guys who don't shave, who smell like goats and dress like refugees from one end of the year to the other, were out there tonight in tuxedos and red or black ties. With fresh haircuts, they really cut a handsome swath. The girls, who usually look like Russian factory workers, with their oversized black shoes, hair tied up with bubble gum and wrapping paper, and foul tongues that would make a George Carlin or a Lenny Bruce wince, were absolutely beautiful. They had their cocktail dresses or evening gowns on; some even wore corsages, had lipstick and rouge, and were neatly coiffed. One couple was in drag. They were hilarious. In an American school, they probably wouldn't even have stood out, but here they were considered a bit odd. I think the faculty who had dropped by enjoyed them more than the other students did. Perhaps it's the sophistication level. The young lady in question came over to me at one point and asked if I could tie her bow tie (they're called "dickie bows" here). I had to stand behind her to do it. I muffed a couple times, then tried it backwards, standing in front of her. After a few stabs, we got it right to the delight of the crowd. They burst into applause.

We stopped at a soccer pitch near home to watch the neighborhood kids play. Kate was supposedly the only girl participant. As I drove up, we could see her flush. Our presence was not very welcome.

In a crisp Irish stage whisper, I heard her say, "Hey lads, put out the fags (cigarettes) and hide the beer and drugs."

She wasn't in the match, but when I suggested she should be, she agreed and called one of the boys who was. Said she'd like to join in.

He looked at her quizzically, and responded, "We're already losing. What do we need you for?"

I couldn't contain my laughter. Kate was mad and suggested we leave. We did.

Saturday, May 1. Because of her sore hand, Kate took a "pass" on riding today. The reins would have been too hard to handle.

Mary and I spent a good deal of time at the kitchen table over coffee discussing the past year and what it had meant to each of us. Although Kate doesn't pass up an opportunity to tell us how much she hates Ireland, and how she wants to go home, the truth is she's never been busier nor had a fuller social calendar, never had such a year of growth or freedom of movement, and never enjoyed more novel experiences than this year. She will have some adjusting to do back in the States. She will be able to handle it, but the return to a venal, pressurized society will be tough.

Mary and I, both together and separately, have had the greatest social life since our early, married days. I've opened up doors I couldn't even find before, and she has been like a missionary preaching on the fringes of civilization about early childhood education. Our lives have been criss-crossed by an amazingly wide variety of characters and character studies, and this place is chock full of both.

Since I had left a few reference works in my office, I had to drive in to school in the afternoon. There were a few dozen cars and coaches parked along the roadside as I pulled through the campus gate. I was curious as to what was going on, so I parked the car and started walking in the direction of some shouting voices. There was an American softball game in progress among about fifteen students. The kids had all the lingo down:

"Slide! Slide!"

"This one's an easy out."

"It's mine."

"The count is zero and two."

"Low and Outside."

"Pick him off."

I suppose most of them had only seen the game on TV, but they obviously enjoyed it. I stayed for a couple of innings. Then I heard a crowd roaring from another direction over a knoll.

When I walked over the rise, I discovered a brand new oval with eight lanes and a cast of several hundred. It was the Irish Special Olympics. Typically, there hadn't been a word about it in the papers. Almost everything in this small country is advertised by word of mouth.

It was a real heartwarming, and at times, tear-provoking experience for me. I had never seen the Games in person. The dedication of the staff and trainers, the exuberance and confidence and joy of the participants, and the quiet pride of the parents and families lent a very special aura. The entrants were racing and shot-putting while I was there. Young and old alike, they were innocent and guileless in their approach to the events. They laughed, hammed it up, gave victory signs. Some could barely walk, let alone run or throw, but they were thoroughly engaged. Eunice Kennedy was right on target focusing, funding, and inspiring these Games worldwide.

After dinner, we repaired to the den. I had built up a tremendous fire earlier. This has been typical of our experience here. No television, no radio in the evening. When we've been home, the program has consisted mostly of the fire, reading, and conversation.

Sunday, May 12. I suggested this morning that Mary and Kate put their travel preferences on the table, since time is getting short before our departure. Mary would like to get up to the North, but Kate doesn't want to GO ANYWHERE. "Who wants to look at piles of stones that used to be houses, or stare at historical blades of grass?" So much for culture and the twelve-year-old.

We took a leisurely stroll up to Mass and stopped at Tommy McNamara's garden. Tommy was already out pruning and nursing. He came over to share some of his latest breedings, a bunch of perfectly beautiful reddish blue-black, almost magenta, tulips. He called them "Black nuns." With a twinkle, he said he was working on some "Black priests," but hadn't had any luck yet.

We took a drive up to Nenagh in the afternoon to arrange a Mass for the mother of a dear friend of ours from back home, Judy Howard. Judy's mom, Josie, whom we also knew well, had been raised in Nenagh.

On the way home, we ran into one of those "only in Ireland" situations. A herd of cows had got out of the field and were wandering around the middle of the Dublin Road, the main artery through this part of the country. Traffic simply came to a standstill, and was backed up for miles until the cows could be lured back in to their pastures. I didn't even hear one horn tooted or one driver's curse throughout the event. The whole affair was taken in stride. The "no problem" syndrome.

I walked up to Finnegan's to drop off some biographical material to Jimmy Hassett. He's still checking out the Kilkee connection on the Gorman clan. Alan O'Reilly walked in and he was in a very talkative mood. Alan only drinks soda water and lime, thereby belying the "Irish myth." He comes to the pub every night with his brothers to talk and listen to the gossip. He told me the Irish people spend about ninety percent of their time talking about one another. It's a small community and there aren't many diversions.

I wish I'd had a tape recorder that night because many of his observations were gems. I asked about one clan and he proceeded through the whole family, a family who lived and bred (and bred and bred) over on the Shannon and who'd been on the dole for years. Then he looked down the bar to another guy whose father simply disappeared several years ago, leaving the mother to play the field and a few kids who ran off with people who had the misfortune to be married already. And then there was the couple who had been on the dole for years, but who nonetheless dress up every night and go have several pints at the Castle Oaks Hotel.

Erskine Caldwell would have had a field day right here in this bar. There is enough material in the neighborhood for two "Tobacco Roads"— the incest, the running around, the welfare cheating, the idiocy, the Jukes and Kallicuks.

Just to add to the color of the place tonight, Willy Cosgrove, a local electrician, appeared. Like the cows, Willy's mule, Francis, also had gotten loose today and wandered onto the Dublin Road. Willy had to go get him. The mule kicked Willy. Not to be outdone, Willy kicked the mule in the head and damn near killed him.

Monday, May 13. I met with Nick Rees to go over the "drill" for tomorrow's joint lecture.
The rest of the day was spent on telephone calls, correspondence, and paper work.

Tuesday, May 14. I lectured the fourth year International Relations undergraduates this afternoon. It was a two-hour program. Nick opened and closed on a theoretical note, and I filled in all the practical, relevant insights. The students really enjoyed the lecture. It was most enjoyable for me as well. I took them through the structure of the U.S. Federal Government, the various influences on foreign policymaking, and the current sources of stress in US-EC relations.

Nick and I went over to the Stables for a post-mortem and ran into an old friend, Professor Jan Van Putten from the Free University of Amsterdam. Jan had just completed a lecture on trade relations between the EC and Russia. It was quite a coincidence. We compared lots of notes and discussed the business and political climate in Eastern Europe.

After dinner, I took a stroll up to Finnegan's and fell into a conversation with Eamon Lawler.

We talked about the party system in Ireland. He told me there was no real philosophical difference between the two major parties. They just followed different leaders. He felt the parties would go the way of the flesh if they ever realigned along ideological grounds.

When I mentioned that I was going to Belfast tomorrow, he made a curious admission.

"I've never been across the Border. I dunno. Just never felt comfortable going up there. I might go if I had the right person taking me."

It made me wonder how many others are in his shoes.

Wednesday, May 15. We were all up early this morning. Kate left for school and Mary took me to Colbert Station. I left for Dublin on the 8:30.

It was a pleasant enough trip. I read and wrote. The fields and hills have become much more green and lush since my last trip to Dublin. We stopped at Thurles, Ballybrophy, and Portloaise. I hadn't realized before how the countryside is dotted with abandoned Church of Ireland churches. They had a "lock" on many of the faithful (or unfaithful?) during the Anglo-Irish Ascendancy, but their adherents are like hen's teeth in the Republic today.

There are also hundreds of abandoned cottages and farmhouses in the rural areas and, correspondingly, every town we went through had hundreds of ticky-tacky (Pete Seeger's term) council houses. The flight to the towns was massive, if one didn't go to the US, the UK, or Australia.

After arriving at Heuston Station, I took the bus up to Connolly Station and checked my bags. Then I headed off in the general direction of the Gresham Hotel. I stopped in for a visit to St. Mary Major, the Pro-Cathedral. There's an interesting dimension to many of the cathedrals in Ireland. When the Protestants took control, of course the cathedrals became prime objects of expropriation. When the Catholics regained power, they built new Cathedrals, called them Pro-Cathedrals, and left the old ones in the hands of the Church of Ireland.

St. Patrick's Cathedral is the seat of the Bishop of the Church of Ireland; St. Mary Major is the Catholic throne.

The train left Connolly Station a couple minutes after one o'clock under scattered clouds. The Metro (weather service) had predicted rain in the North this afternoon. We passed through some pretty poor, rundown neighborhoods, but the front doors of almost all the houses—the Doors of Dublin—were painted in bright colors!

About ten minutes out of the station, the conductor came by to announce that we would have to get off the train at Dundalk and take a bus to Newry. There had been a bomb scare. He went from seat to seat with the news. Most of the passengers hardly reacted. Two women went on with their conversation, a priest across the aisle continued saying the Rosary, the fellow in the seat in front of me simply rolled over and went back to sleep. And I sat there shaking. Frankly, I'd never been through a bomb threat before.

In about forty-five minutes, we reached Drougheda and the River Boyne. I was terribly disappointed. This had been the site of a decisive military battle between the forces of William of Orange and James II in 1690. The River now was full of freighters. There was nothing to indicate the historical significance of the place. (Although the defeat of the Jacobites solidified British rule in Ireland and precipitated an era of repression unparalleled in Irish history, it is ironic that the composition of both opposing armies was overwhelmingly Irish.)

When we stopped at Dundalk, I asked the stationmaster who was responsible for the bomb threat.

"Who else? he said. "The I . . . R . . . A . . ."

We transferred to a tour coach, and I asked the fellow sitting next to me how often these incidents occur.

"It depends, "he said," on how often they decide to blow up the tracks—perhaps once or twice a week."

Dundalk is a pretty town. It reminds one of a New England village, complete with a tree-lined commons.

The frontier between the North and the Republic lies in a mountain valley. We slowed down, but the coach never stopped. I asked my seat-mate if that was all there was to crossing the border. He said the control point was up ahead.

It was literally an armed camp—bunkers, sandbags, cement fortifications, sixteen-millimeter guns, barbed wire, and British Specials everywhere armed with Tommy guns and automatic carbines. There was a huge sign forbidding photographs. My mind wandered back to a day at Belleek in County Fermanagh five years ago.

A British soldier there had threatened to shoot me for taking a picture of the guardhouses at the border. The authorities on both sides are terrified that guards and soldiers will be identified from photos and then blackmailed into compromising border security.

When the coach came to a halt, two young Brits boarded, in full battle regalia. They wore camouflage combat uniforms, their faces were greased black and they had guns at the ready. It was scary. One stood right next to me. They didn't do anything but talk with the train conductor who was riding with us, but their armament looked awfully menacing. They couldn't have been more than nineteen or twenty-years-old, and I was nervous that they might get nervous—and shoot someone.

As we got off the coach in Newry, my fellow traveler said this wouldn't have happened if we'd been on an Irish train. It seems the train we were on is owned by the British, and any disruption costs them money. Very simple.

The train ride from Newry into Belfast was uncomplicated but uncomfortable. The carriage was springless and swung from side to side as well. Only three cars.

Paul Arthur was waiting for me when I detrained at the Central Belfast Station. He said he'd had a change in schedule and apologized for the fact that he had to do a TV commentary that night on the London talks (on the North). Hoped I'd understand. Would I like to come along?

We drove up to the Arthurs' house in Bangor, which overlooks Belfast Lough from a bluff. Belfast is one of the largest deep-water ports in the world and a prized possession in the British maritime empire. The vista from Bangor is breathtaking, particularly at sunset.

The TV studio was full of politicians. I felt more than a twinge of nostalgia for my old campaign days.

About midnight, a cab picked us up. The driver expressed great concern over his colleagues being lured into shootings. That is a favorite pastime of the paramilitaries nowadays. They call a cab, knowing that the driver is a Catholic, or a Protestant, and then, depending on their own persuasion, shoot the guy. Great sport. He said he drives nights, but only accepts contract work—such as his contract with the TV station. He won't risk the streets. He said the names on the cabs are a dead giveaway: so and so is a Catholic company, such and such is Protestant, and each is fair game. He had suggested to the cab Commission that they go to numbers, as in the States, Canada, and England, but no one picked up on his recommendation. It's a very dodgy business cabbing after dark in Belfast.

Thursday, May 16. Paul and I went in to Queen's University. I wanted to pay my respects to Prof. Con O'Leary, the Dean of Irish political scientists.

The University was founded in 1857, about the time Belfast was coming into political and economic prominence. There's probably a great deal of "local history" behind its establishment—need for cultural cachet, etc.—but I didn't have an opportunity to pick up any details. The buildings, or at least the original architecture, are Tudor Gothic in rust colored bricks. The filigrees, inlays and epis are magnificent. The yard is filled with fruit trees.

Unfortunately, Con was not in his office, so we went on our way.

Paul suggested that we go down to Sandy Row. The locals, he said, contend that Sandy Row is the actual heart of the British Empire. It is several blocks long, the epicenter of Unionism in the North. We stopped in front of Orange Hall (headquarters of the Orange Order). I was tempted to take a picture, but didn't want to call that much attention to myself. There is always someone watching, and they know an outsider in a second. Paul said there had been occasions where "rogue elephants" had walked into pubs and sprayed strangers—Al Capone style. All this, of course, was designed to make me feel comfortable as we walked through the guts of Orange country.

We reached an intersection and I spotted the Union Jack painted on the side of a building. Paul told me it was the DUP headquarters (Ian Paisley's Party). There was a huge sign that read "Keep Ulster British." Again, I was tempted to take out the camera. Again I passed.

Paul said there was one particular place he wanted to take me—the Hotel Europa. It sounded rather quaint until he told me it was the most heavily bombed building in Belfast. Only last week a bomb had gone off on the seventh floor. No injuries—intentionally—just psychological warfare.

As we entered the lobby, I was carrying my black overnight bag and every eye in the place immediately focused on the bag. I said laughingly that they probably thought I had a bomb in the bag.

He said, "Don't laugh! Even in a suit and tie, you could be a thug. After all, thugs aren't supposed to look like thugs when they come in here."

That put a whole different spin on the situation.

We walked into the bar and sat at a table. I slid the bag under and started for the bathroom, then thought better of it.

If I left the bag under the table and Paul happened to get up for any reason, we would probably both be nabbed. If I took the bag to the bathroom, I certainly would have been followed. I just sat there and almost wet my pants.

Several armored cars with howitzers (or some type of mount) passed in front of the hotel almost unnoticed by the pedestrians. The nonchalance was interesting.

A pub across the street looked as though it were being torn down. The two top floors were already pretty well demolished. Paul told me they had been blown off by a bomb explosion about three weeks ago. The roaring hell of this town was beginning to register.

After a brief rest, we continued our journey toward the business district. As we approached the City Square and shopping mall on Royal Street, I was impressed with the rebuilding and renovation that had taken place. In spite of all the trouble, people are beginning to reinvest in the heart of town.

The Square (Donegall Square, named for Lord Donegall) is dominated by City Hall, a beautiful late Victorian edifice. The building, unfortunately, can only be entered by invitation or pass. It is surrounded by an iron fence, which, of course, is secured and patrolled. How's that for democracy in action!

Directly across the street from City Hall was something I'd never seen in my life. A privately-owned, membership subscription-funded library. The Linen Hall Library. It was a marvelous old place with creaky stairs, burnished floors, reading rooms, a refectory, and miles and miles of bookracks. An exquisite collection. Membership is, I believe, open to anyone, but it is not a 'public' library in the sense that Americans use the term. The name is derived from the linen industry, which served for decades as the economic underpinning for modern Belfast.

We walked around the corner to Royal Street, the heart of retail Belfast. It is a pleasant broadway converted to a pedestrian mall—like Amsterdam, or Grafton Street in Dublin—except that there is a two-story high iron gate at all the access points through which everyone must pass. Every bus or delivery van that goes through is searched. I stood there in utter amazement as the police conducted their searches not twenty feet from me. They did not touch anyone or demand any IDs, but they were fearsome just by their presence. The public, I suspect, welcomes that presence, however.

We made a couple of ritual pub stops for some local color and then walked over to the Botanic Garden Station where Margaret met us with my suitbag. I caught the 3:00 back to Dublin. I had packed a hell of a lot into less than twenty-four hours, and had come away with quite an education.

Friday, May 17. I was up early this morning and went in to the library to do some research for my lecture to Coakley's students. It was appalling to find exactly ONE reference work on the shelves!

Tried writing frequently during the day, but the images from yesterday's trip kept cluttering up my mind and I never finished more than a handful of unconnected notes.

Saturday, May 18. With a little bit of discipline, I managed to complete at least an outline and an approach for Monday's lecture. Still, it's tough to flesh out material for students who can only relate to the United States in abstractions or through correspondence from an emigrant cousin.

Compounding all this pressure, of course, is the fact that I still have to prepare two lectures for John Stapleton's Public Administration class (I don't even know the subject or the dates at this point), one more lecture for Nick Rees (don't know the subject there either), and a major, two-hour lecture for Dr. Whelan's History Seminar—all within the next two weeks.

As of today, Coakley has yet to give me the context for Monday's program. It reminds me of the days when I used to "wing it." I can do it, but it's more stressful now.

Sunday, May 19. Fianna Fail was out in front of church today taking up its annual national collection. It's one of the great phenomena of the country. Every organization, whether it is political, social, eleemosynary, athletic, religious, or what have you, takes up a collection outside the churches at some point in the year. It is all coordinated with the diocese. Today, it was Fianna Fail's turn.

Eamon Lawlor was there, so I stopped to tell him of my Belfast venture. Of course, my observations firmed up all his convictions about never crossing the border. The others there obviously hadn't been "over" either. Most had never been any farther north than County Tipperary. They all stood there gaping at the story of the British soldiers on the bus.

In the afternoon, Kate and I spent a couple of fun-filled hours playing "catch" with only one glove, and scrub soccer without sneakers or cleats. Fortunately, the neighbors didn't know the difference and there were no Americans watching.

Monday, May 20. Mary drove me to the University and I went directly to John Coakley's office. There were a few minor issues I wanted to get straightened away: where the lecture was, what time, and how it was to fit into the context of his other lectures. I had written a very substantive but flexible piece. John has about 30 students in that particular class, including some adults from the Peace Studies program.

The classroom had no lectern, so I had to sit at a desk. It was difficult. I prefer to stand and walk while I'm lecturing, but I had so many points to get across that I really couldn't afford to get too far from my notes, and failing eyes wouldn't allow me to read off the desk from a standing position. Simple mechanical issues like this can be critical to the delivery of a good message.

I took the class through a history of Irish migration to the States, destroyed the myth about the Irish-American community being Catholic, developed the theme of Anglo-Irish relations and the subsequent impact on U.S. relations with Ireland, and portrayed both the emergence and the decline of an Irish-American political elite. I had the distinct impression that most of my remarks were new information to everyone in the room. Even John admitted there was a lot of material of which he'd been unaware.

The lecture and the question period ran close to two hours. I was very pleased.

Two of the gentlemen I had met at the Cork County Council during my cooperative education visit, Dahai Heroun and John Kennedy, were in town today with Jerry Cronin. I joined them over at the Stables late in the afternoon.

They are all Corkmen ("Cokmin," as they call themselves) and so the conversation was not only very witty, but mostly unintelligible to the average ear. We ranged up and down the political ladder. Two were Fianna Fail men and one was a Laborite. They were all somewhat fascinated by my interpretation of the Parties in Ireland, and the moral state of the Government (which is at low ebb these days). We discussed the dissimilarities between their highly centralized system and U.S. federalism. Cities and counties have virtually no power here, only administrative authority. They seemed intrigued at our level of diversity and at the prospect of actually being able to DO something. They are all members of a union, all employees of the State, and are paid from the same scale.

Tuesday, May 21. It was still gray and gloomy this morning. The natives say it is one of the worst Mays in recent years. "Summer's almost over," one said. I almost threw up at that thought.

I spent a lot of time drafting longhand notes for my History Seminar lecture. I'm still not settled on my approach. The topic is "Politics: An American Perspective." There are a half dozen ways to get at it. I am writing at this point to see where it will take me.

The campus is lush now. All the shrubbery is in full foliage and only a few trees remain unfilled. If it weren't for the absolutely ugly entrance to the main building—it looks like it was designed and constructed with an Erector Set—the aesthetics would be perfect. There are long, tree-lined driveways up to the building complex, replete with at least a dozen types of flowers and flowering bushes—primrose, gorse, violets, etc. Plassey House faces out on a broad lawn sloping down to the River Shannon. The House is early Victorian in starched white, set off by red azaleas. The landscaping is creative and meticulously groomed.

Wednesday, May 22. The order of the day for me was disciplined writing in the kitchen. I chose that venue because Kate was at school and Mary was off to the Burren with the University wives group for a day of hiking and exploring. Unlike the office, the house was suitably quiet.

I noticed that night when Kate came in from jogging that the sun had just barely set. It was ten o'clock!

Thursday, May 23. For the first time this year, I cranked open the windows in my office this morning. The air was absolutely perfumed by Mayflowers. They're everywhere in Ireland. Large bushes (almost trees) with delicate white blossoms, they smell somewhat like rose petals. I'd always thought of them as generic—flowers that blossomed in May—rather than as a specific flower.

Despite the redolence, the beauty, and the sun, I did manage to squeeze in a good bit of time thinking and writing.

Friday, May 24. The History Seminar is beginning to get to me. I can't seem to get a focus on exactly what I want to do. The Library is devoid of any reference works on the subject and I'm frustrated because I want to make this a scholarly paper. I've already written several pages of notes, but have yet to string them together. Each day I run into someone new who says, "I can't wait to hear your lecture," and it sends a cold chill up and down my spine.

After lunch, I hopped a double-decker bus into town for a meeting with Garda Inspector Tom Keating. He was helping me iron out a couple of immigration matters.

As frequently happens in this country, we sat and talked politics and history for close to an hour. He was very articulate and snappily dressed in herringbone sport coat, slacks and tie. He's a little jaded by all those years in Gestapo work, but very pleasant and a great conversationalist.

He told me one story about World War II, which I'd never heard. During training off the Devon coast in 1944 (in preparation for D-Day), the Germans surfaced with two E-Boats and wreaked havoc on LSTs and LCTs as well as the cover ships. The Americans panicked and started to return fire—with no real targets. In the end, the E-Boats got away, most of the Allied ships were either sunk or disabled, and several thousand Americans were dead in the water. It never made the press, of course, and apparently has never been verified because of the British Official Secrets Act. Keating felt the men were "officially" killed during the D-Day landing on June 4. It's a fascinating story if it can be proved.

Mary and I ran into Jimmy Hassett at Finnegan's that evening. He hadn't had much luck on the Gorman/O'Gorman genealogy yet, but promised to keep trying.

Jimmy started talking about Kilkee, a seaside resort popular with Limerick vacationers, and about Fanny O'Dea's, an oasis in Lissycasey where shore-goers stop for a break. He said Fanny has a special drink made of whisky and beaten eggs. When I asked him what it was called, he pled ignorance, but said it would make the lads want to "bull a cow." His face lit up at this and he roared with laughter. So did everyone within earshot.

Several of the neighbors stopped over to say hello. We are accepted as real people. It's a nice feeling behind the hedgerows.

Saturday, May 25. There's been a phenomenon in the sky for the last of couple days. While the moon is visible during the day (which in itself is not odd), it is only about three-quarters full. Now, I know the earth's shadow creates the illusion of a crescent, half, or three quarter moon, but if the sun is shining brightly at the same time as the moon, and the earth is obviously not interposed, what causes the impression of less than a full moon? There is no earth shadow. I've looked at a couple of source works and can't find an answer. It probably has something to do with our being so far into the Northern Hemisphere (Ireland is only six hundred miles from the Arctic Circle), but it's a mystery to me.

Kate came home from Ashroe bubbling over. She had cantered beautifully, and had done several successful high jumps. She rode "Isabel," and the horse responded readily to her. She looked like a sixteen-year-old in her long point shirt, flowing hair, black boots and riding pants. Casual chic.

She strode across the lawn toward me and called, "Pop, you'd have been proud of me."

You bet I would.

It was a warm but overcast day, the type that induces spring fever.

Sunday, May 26. After biking in to Ryan's for the papers, we all ambled our way up the road to 11:00 Mass at Ahane. Tommy McNamara's garden was resplendent with rose-purple columbine, primroses, and Chinese lanterns, whose blossoms looked like vaulted orange lampshades.

The sermon was worse than usual. At one point, Fr. Minogue actually took time to have the congregation meticulously and articulately make the sign of the cross.

"Now, let's try it. In the name of the Father..."

I felt as though I were back with Sister Cleophas at St. James in 1945. (Several months ago Fr. Minogue had unburdened himself of a lecture on the proper way to genuflect.) There was nothing about the faith—just the rituals. I doubt that he had the serious attention of anyone in the church under twenty-five. It was a pathetic throwback to the Ireland of the past. "Just be humble and ignorant, and we'll tell you what to do."

While the parish announcements were being made, I was struck by the collection figures. Last week, this dirt-poor little church had forked over almost five hundred pounds (eight hundred dollars) for the Maynooth Seminary and several hundred more for the parish priest collection. Giving and sharing are fundamental to life here.

We stopped to chat with our neighbors, Pat and Sadie McGrath, on the way out of church.

Pat is a painting contractor. He said his business is down this year—purposely. Last year, he paid X dollars in corporation taxes and fifty-four percent in income taxes. By taking in less business this year, he will halve his corporate tax, he'll have more time to play golf, and he won't be employing someone who is currently on the dole.

"Why should I kill myself?" he said. "The government simply takes the money and hands it to someone who won't work. There's no incentive for me, and no way I can build up my capital."

His frustration over the current tax structure is felt all over the country, I fear.

Monday, May 27. This was a busy day for everyone. Kate was cramming for exams, Mary was working on a paper, and I had all sorts of phone calls and paperwork. John Stapleton dropped in and asked me to do an impromptu lecture on lobbying for his Public Administration class in the morning.

In the evening, with the girls still very engaged in their projects, I went for a long bike ride—up Clyduff Road, past the Ahane church to the back lane and down along the hedgerows. I stopped to take in the landscape. It was spectacular. I could look down through a boreen across the fields for miles. The patchwork quilt of the hedge-separated fields was magnificent. The sun was relatively high (it was a little past 8:00), but there were enough shadows to give it a restful, pastoral look. Dairy cows everywhere, of course. Off to the north were the Silvermines Mountains in County Tipperary. The breeze was from the northeast, so the clouds looked as though they had sprung forth from the mountains. Big pink and cream puffballs, at first peaking, and then leaping, over the hilltops.

Tuesday, May 28. Mary had to drive Kate in to school, because apparently the schools are all on different exam schedules this week and, as they say here with characteristic Irish understatement, the bus service is "erratic."

About twenty students showed up with John Stapleton for my lecture. I guided them through the various levels of government in the U.S., the lack of party discipline in Congress (and most state legislatures, for that matter), the actual legislative process and the role of lobbyists in that process. I only used a handful of notes and props. Although it was a clinical analysis of the American system, it was also highly anecdotal, which lent some personal coloration.

I always enjoy sharing my insights and experiences with the students.

When dinner was over, I walked across the street to Jim and Niamh O'Sullivan's. I had noticed Jim painting the trim on the house and decided to go over and have a chat. I'd only had one serious conversation with him since last September. He always seemed to be working nights (he's in the Garda) and he was never around, so they didn't socialize much.

Jim is a very articulate guy with an obvious grasp of the politics, the ethics, and the power structure in Ireland. He's a Corkman who transferred here because of employment.

He said that in his childhood the priests in his hometown in Cork were absolutely dictatorial. When the lads wanted to use the rec hall for indoor soccer during the winter, they were refused. The parish priest blocked it because soccer was a "foreign" game. Over and over, I've picked up that theme. The Church, Fianna Fail, and the GAA.

Wednesday, May 29. I wrote feverishly today and actually got a great deal accomplished.

I remembered around dinnertime that John O'Brien from Crescent School had told me I should try to stop by the Liszt concert and chat with Fr. Dermot Murray, the Headmaster. I was about to leave when a huge water fight broke out in the neighborhood, involving all the kids. It was hilarious and everyone got soaked. There are no outdoor spigots or garden hoses around here, so everyone had to run into houses, fill cans or bottles or whatever, and then go after the enemy. Kids leapt over walls, ducked, bobbed and screamed. It was like my old neighborhood growing up, but unlike anything Kate had ever experienced. God, she will miss this place!

I finally drove over to Crescent about 9:30. Ironically, the Liszt Orchestra played only Mozart and Mendelssohn—a very Irish quality.

Dermot greeted me very warmly with "Hello, Professor." He said Kate's application was all a matter of numbers. There were currently two vacancies and Kate was number three on the list.

Then, as an afterthought, he added, "Did you see the parents' poll? Ninety-five percent of the parents in Limerick said if they had a preference, they'd have their kids educated at Crescent."

I gathered that was an indication of how much of a favor I was going to owe him. Subtle Jesuits!

I stopped at Finnegan's for a couple minutes and Alan O'Reilly invited me to go up to a Tipperary stud farm with him on Friday. That should be an eye-opener. It's a very significant invitation into the local farmers' "world."

Thursday, May 30. I turned my hand to writing this morning. The History Seminar lecture was still all over the lot. I had notes, thoughts, even whole paragraphs that were unconnected and, in some instances, unrelated.

Dabbled at my paper throughout the day with only mild success.

Friday, May 31. After a restless night, I surfaced about 5:30. It was a magnificent, cloudless day. Still cool at that hour—like Florida in the winter and Lake Ontario in the summer—but promising to be perfect. I had a good hardy breakfast (I had been warned to eat well because of the long day ahead), put on slacks, a casual shirt and a sport coat.

Alan O'Reilly picked me up a little later. He had a horse van attached to the car. Mary enquired as to when we might be home.

"Maybe two hours. Maybe 6:00. It depends on 'your man.' "

"Your man", of course, is the Irish version of "the guy."

The car was a sight to behold. It made our blue bomb look like a chariot. There was so much mud on the windshield I could barely see the road. Most of the door handles were broken and both front windows had to be pulled up and shoved down by hand. No rollers.

We stopped at a farm in Castleconnell owned by Dick "Mac" Ryan. ("Mac" distinguished him from the two hundred other Dick Ryans in the area.). We loaded on a beautiful gray mare and her nine-day-old foal, a colt, and then the three of us started north on the Dublin Road into County Tipperary.

We drove through Nenagh and off toward Borrisokane. Just outside, we turned down the road to Carney. It was lush countryside and very serene.

We came to a one-lane road, opened the gate and started in. Alan leaned on the horn to warn anyone coming toward us and I soon learned why. The road is about a mile long, winding and rutted. It is the width of a car with perhaps one foot to spare. Backing up, particularly with a van attached, would have been sheer hell. We made it, leaning on the horn all the way.

The stud farm has no name. It is simply Philip Heenan's place. No outdoor lights (although they frequently work till midnight). No telephone. No place to eat or drink. It was so isolated that, with the exception of the rumble of horse vans, the sounds were all natural.

It was somewhere around 10:30 when we got there. Heenan greeted Alan warmly, was correct with Ryan, and ignored me altogether. Alan told him about me, though.

The whole place consisted of an abandoned farmhouse, an old stucco shed, and two cement block buildings with stalls. Heenan keeps ten or twelve stallions around, but he only used four while we were there.

There were probably a dozen or so men and boys hanging around. One fellow was standing with a mare on a tether, holding her up to a window where a pony poked its face out. At that point, I hadn't a clue what the rhythm of the place was or what to expect. All of a sudden, Heenan said to the guy with the mare, "Take her up." The fellow started to lead the horse up a dirt driveway to a wide clearing. Everyone else fell in behind at a dogtrot. The place began to buzz. When we got to the clearing, a chap named Ned Ryan Og (Young Ned), who was some sort of assistant, was carefully looping ropes around the hind legs of the mare. The ropes were then joined together with a larger rope that had been laid over the mare's back and wrapped around her torso. They were tied firmly and knotted at the side of the neck. It was called 'hobbling,' a term I'd heard a thousands times, but never understood until today. The obvious purpose was to keep the mare from kicking.

A pole with a hook on it was stuck in the side of the mare's mouth and the hook wrapped around her tongue. This was used to quiet her down. Two tether lines were pulled in opposite directions by volunteers.

At that point, Heenan appeared, leading a stallion. A beautiful chestnut. The mare was a roan. He walked the stud around behind the mare. The stud began sniffing and nibbling at her buttocks. Then, like clockwork, he had an erection. It was the damnedest thing to watch. All I could think of was a submarine periscope, only this went straight out rather than up. The stallion rose up and "covered" the mare, as they say here. Heenan nonchalantly guided the penis in. The whole program took about fifteen seconds. He walked the stallion away.

They unhobbled the mare, and then with a single tether, one fellow walked her around for about five minutes. He took her back to her van and that was that. Everybody went back to their old stations and stood around waiting and talking.

I felt comfortable enough to start asking questions by then. The ponies in the stables, the ones who nuzzle and lick the mares, are called "teasers." They are used to determine if the mare is "on" or "in season," as the saying goes. This is the equine equivalent of being "in heat."

If the pony pays attention to the mare, and starts chewing at her or licking her vulva, or if the mare pays particular attention to the pony, she is ready. Heenan's trained eye determines who's "on" and who isn't. He simply sends people home if their mare isn't ready.

Heenan is quite a character. He says he's seventy, although he looked no more than mid-fifties. He wore an old cap, herringbone sport coat, non-descript shirt, dirty pants, and black work boots with red laces. He had a pleasant, almost impish face. He was dropping 'pearls' all over the place, to the delight of everyone. A real showman—although he is obviously also one of the best in his business.

I saw pictures of robins and titwillows eating out of his hand and while we were hanging around between "coverings," he had one dog in his lap and two others at his feet. A regular Francis of Assisi. His studs' overall fertility rate is eighty percent, and some stallions go as high as ninety-three percent. Most stud managers, I am told, would give anything to maintain a sixty-percent rate.

A while later I got bold and took a picture of him with "Tiny," the Jack Russell in his lap.

He looked at me and said, "Very arrogant."

I thought for a minute he'd throw the three of us out. He had a cantankerous reputation.

"Yes, very arrogant of him, eh, Tiny?" and he laughed.

It meant he had accepted me after several hours of observing.

Without any notice, he was up again and directing the next man with a mare to "take her up." The program was repeated. Again and again, as FDR used to say. Still no signs when he would take us, though, and there were many who came after us who had already been serviced.

It was quite warm now, and Alan was getting agitated. "Are you sure you made an appointment with him, Dick?"

"Absolutely! Told him we'd be here Friday morning."

There was some speculation at that point about Philip's "failing memory." After listening to him and his recounting of almost every mare he had handled and almost every filly or colt that had been foaled, and when certain mares were due, I had serious doubts about his "failing memory," however. I had the distinct impression that he thought Alan had simply brought me up to observe. Nothing had been said about the mare, and of course, we hadn't let the mare and colt out of the van—which was parked in the back of another field. I suggested one of them enquire if he even knew we were waiting.

Dick finally approached him. He was squeamish because Heenan might have said, "Don't like the service? Good-bye!"

Anyway, he went over, and came back with a smile. We'd be done a little after 3:00. It was then 2:30. Philip called over to Alan:

"I thought you were here for a visit, a ride in the country, Alan."

At about 3:10, Heenan called for the mare to be "teased." She was ornery and skittish with her foal alongside. The pony didn't seem interested, either. Still he said, "Take her up." He had seen something.

I came close to walking in front of the mare and Dick said to me, "A horse is dangerous at either end, and suspect in the middle." A great piece of country wisdom.

After the procedure was over, I thanked Heenan for the education and told him I'd send a copy of the picture to "Tiny." Perhaps "Tiny" would share it with him. He chuckled loudly, then headed back to the bench to call up another mare.

Five hours had been fascinating—but plenty. I couldn't imagine anyone spending sixteen hours a day, three hundred and sixty-five days a year helping horses propagate.

Today had been a real eye-opener for me, though. I thoroughly enjoyed myself.

As a premature birthday present to Kate, I took a carload of girls from the neighborhood up to a disco in Newport after dinner. I waited in Gleeson's pub on the village square. I was, frankly, a little nervous. It was a first for Kate and I didn't know anything about the crowd that would be there. The evening came off without a hitch, however.

Saturday, June 1. Kate and I went to Ashroe this morning where she rode "Isabel" again. It was a good day.

On the way back, we stopped at the grocery store in Newport and, lo and behold, the first person I ran into was Ned Ryan Og. We had a fine chat about yesterday. He said it is almost mysterious the way Philip Heenan handles animals. Those old stallions are dangerous—literally—but he goes into the stables and talks to them and they do what he wants. He also talks to birds, dogs, trees, you name it. As we were standing there, a waitress from Gleeson's stopped to say hello. Although I'd just met her last night, she knew Ned quite well. Then Patti Punch drove up. The loops in this country are getting smaller and smaller for me.

Since our journey is slowly coming to an end at this point, Mary and I decided in the afternoon to drive up to Glenstal Abbey and take some pictures for our scrapbook.
The winding driveway up to the Abbey castle is lined at this time of year with pink, purple, red, and magenta rhododendron bushes and a local flavor of azalea. They were obviously past peak today, but still magnificent.

We wandered around in the silence of the place, through pathways, under bowers, up to the tiered Italian garden, over through the cemetery. The grounds are covered with stately cedar trees. There is an immense lily pond and even an old stone arched bridge over a gurgling creek.

Everywhere we went, there were fuchsia, rhododendron, velvet slippers, primroses, and flowers and bushes I'd never seen before. The odors were out of this world, and the place was alive with honeybees hovering all over the berry bushes. At one point the only sounds we heard were from the bees. Occasionally, we saw a monk walking along reading his breviary, or a visiting nun just sitting, contemplating. Talk about getting away from it all!

The ride back was brilliant. We took the high road over through Newport and the hills were absolutely resplendent with color. Purple and pink rhododendron trees by the thousands, interspersed with yellow and green gorse bushes and the lilac heather. This panorama went on for miles up into the surrounding hillsides and along the road. I was gaping so much, I almost drove over the edge.

Sunday, June 2. The temperature dropped considerably overnight. It was cool and overcast with a good stiff breeze out of the northwest. It even misted over, for the first time in about ten days. We had given serious thought to driving over to Listowel in County Kerry for the Writers' Week Festival and perhaps catching John B. Keane's "Big Maggie." The idea of plodding over there on wet back roads didn't do much for me, though.

Mass was a little different today. The celebrant was a Jesuit from Boston, and the sermon was preached by a Redemptorist from Limerick City. Local lore has it that the Redemptorists were the guiding force behind the movement that drove most of the Jews out of Limerick around the turn of the century. I think it was the only recorded incident of its kind in the history of Ireland. There really is not, nor has there ever been, any serious anti-Semitism in Ireland. At one time, the Lords Mayor of both Dublin and Cork were Jewish. Limerick in the early 1900s, though, was terribly isolated and xenophobic (many of the old-timers still are) and, at the tender mercies of a Father Coughlin-type, the locals could be pretty rough.

Tommy McNamara's spring garden was just about gone, but his gold and red roses were starting to bud. They are actually two-toned. I'm anxious to see them in bloom—probably in a week or so.

The weather had cleared up, so I checked the Writers' Week schedule. There was a traditional Irish music festival in Tralee that sounded like fun. Mary packed a picnic lunch and the three of us headed southwest.

We took the main Cork Road down through Patrickswell (St. Patrick reputedly came here and blessed the well water in the fifth century, hence the name), went on further to Adare, and then turned onto the Tralee-Killarney Road. Down through Rathkeale, Newmarket West and Abbeyfeale, and west over toward Tralee. The weather was beautiful by now, and there was almost no traffic. I pulled off the road once for a grand view of the valley between County Limerick and County Kerry. Its broad sweep was mind-boggling and the visibility must have been forty or fifty miles—all the way to the mountains in the South of Kerry.

Tralee is a fair-sized town. Over the years, there has been a good deal of American investment there (Burlington Industries, e.g.), but nothing seems to have taken hold. Tourists are still the mainstay of the economy.

We stopped in town and after a brief walking tour, headed out to the Dingle Peninsula. In all the times I've been to Ireland, I had never been to Dingle.

As we drove along a tidal backwater toward the harbor, a huge windmill loomed up in front of us. It was the wind-driven generating project the Irish American Partnership had come over to look at last year. It's located at Blennerville at the base of the peninsula. The mill fans were tied down so we didn't see them turning. The operation is still in the test-pattern phase and apparently the mill only functions periodically—like when they get enough money to man it! Considering the stiff Atlantic winds, mills such as this could be a godsend for a power-starved economy.

We headed out the peninsula in the general direction of Mt. Brandon and passed a village named Stradbally. Having checked the map earlier, I knew we were aimed right, but I didn't realize we were supposed to turn at that town. We continued straight on, and the next thing I knew we passed some of the most beautiful beaches I'd seen in Ireland—white sand with great surf—but with no visible access. They were absolutely deserted. Very Irish.

Within minutes of the beaches, I realized that the land mass was jutting further and further to the north and that we were climbing. The mountains were awesome but harsh, and the road was steep and sinewy. There were alternately, hedgerows, small wire fences, and low walls on the downside of the road. This meant that descending cars were constantly crowding on to my side (the left) of the road, which was bounded by a ditch.

I wasn't sure whether the tires or the clutch would go first. The heights were dizzying. We could see clouds covering several of the mountaintops. At one point, I took a quick glance over my shoulder and almost threw up. The scarp on the left and the precipice on the right leading down to the valley and out to the ocean were a bit too much. I hung on to the steering wheel for dear life and left the rest of the rubbernecking to my passengers.

It was now obvious that we had taken the wrong road, but it was equally obvious that we didn't know where we were. My navigator pinpointed us in Conor Pass. About five or six miles up we found a little pull-off and stopped. We were hard beside a rocky scarp—jagged, ominous, and incredibly high—probably another half mile straight up. The view below was almost overwhelming, too. There was some haze down by the water, but the valley stretched clearly for several miles to the shore in one direction and over to the next mountain ridge in the other. Ahead of us, of course, lay the next several miles of narrow mountain road leading up through the Pass.

As we proceeded on what by now had turned into a goat path, a van came down toward us. There was no way we could pass him and no way we could back up. He yielded, and as he moved backward, I stayed nuzzled to his front bumper to discourage him from changing his mind. Luckily there was a widening about five hundred feet above and we passed without incident.

The view from the top of the pass was nothing short of splendid. It was so clear by then that we could look out at Tralee Harbor to the North and down into Dingle Bay on the south and even across to the forbidding rocks of the Ring of Kerry.

We played for a while on the mountaintop—Kate trying to coax me to the edge of the cliff while I turned greener than the scenery.

The road down to Dingle town was straighter, less steep, and topographically different than the Tralee road. Much of the land was arable, with the typical Irish patchwork quilt of fields.

From Dingle, the road ran inland, but at Inch it came back to the Bay with the Ring directly across. I had never expected anything so overpowering. It was a scene people would fly or drive thousands of miles to see, and we were practically alone on the road! The view was like Amalfi, and the Conor Pass had been the Andes without condors or pan whistles. What a travelogue!

Monday, June 3. Today turned into a sort-out, throw-out day. Each of us got into piles, shelves, drawers, etc., and began the torturous process of winnowing. I packed books and spent hours going through my personal papers. For almost ten months, I had simply thrown my financial records into a desk drawer. Now came the reckoning. It was a pain, but a purgative as well.

Kate, who is a genuine packrat, had mountains of things to go through. Mary sorted and packed several boxes of clothes.

This whole situation is exacerbated by the fact that we still don't know where we'll be in September—Ireland, Washington, or New York—or what we will need. Kate, for her part, is learning how to roll with the punches.

Tuesday, June 4. Kate's thirteenth birthday!

The History Seminar, which is geared more to faculty and the public than to the student body, took place in the formal Green Room in Plassey House this afternoon. It was the largest crowd they had all year, which made me feel good. I was particularly pleased that quite a number of students showed up.

I took the audience through the formative stages of the American Union, the divergence of opinion over a powerful Central government, and the subsequent development of our political parties along those lines—up to the 1933 watershed of the New Deal.

Next, I addressed the issue of contemporary American politics and explained the party system and its various manifestations (national, congressional, state, local). Much to their surprise and enjoyment, I shared with the group the strong role played in the American process by our academic community.

Even for a sophisticated audience such as they, my personal observations and anecdotal experiences were a welcome digression from some of the more traditional lectures.

Including several articulate exchanges during a question and answer session, the program ran close to two hours—much longer than usual. Bernadette Whelan and Brian Faloon (the co-chairs) said they were very pleased. So was I.

That night I drove in to town to a twenty-first birthday party, which is sort of a rite of passage in Ireland. It was in honor of Colm Croffy, the President of the Student's Union. I was the only faculty member invited. There must have been two hundred students.

During the course of my visit, probably two-dozen students came up to thank me for a particular lecture, to ask a question, to ask for an appointment, or just to chat. It was very rewarding. I don't think they feel they can talk to most of the other faculty that freely. It's a part of that "brokered" society I have sensed so often here: Don't question; don't doubt. Do as you are told. Americans, on the other hand, are much more open. I believe it's that casual American approach that had put the students at ease.

Wednesday, June 5. Kate had her Math exam this morning (they call it "matts" here, short for mathematics). She and I had really had to struggle with this one.

I had a lecture this morning on U.S.-EC relations. It was with the first year European Integration students, and it was not one of my better performances. There were one hundred and fifty seventeen and eighteen-year-olds in the cavernous Jean Monet theater who really had no background in the subject matter. The material is dry, in and of itself, and I was tired from last night, so the program just plodded along. I could see them drifting, yawning, squirming in their chairs.

Finally, I said, "If you think it's boring out there, you should see what it's like up here trying to make this stuff exciting!"

They laughed out loud and we picked up a little steam. I threw away what modest script I had, and proceeded to go ad lib. I cut the formal lecture short by a few minutes, and then—guts ball—opened it up to a Q & A. Managed to elicit a few good questions, which carried us through. It wasn't a real bomb, but it wasn't exactly a showstopper either.

Nick Rees came in just as I was finishing and we walked out together. I told him I was only halfway happy with myself, and he said:

"I was an absolute disaster yesterday! I was tired, the kids are tired, and they have no capacity to absorb anything new at this point. They simply want to digest what they already learned."

This made me feel a little better about their reaction to my lecture.

We took Kate up to Castleconnell for a belated birthday dinner with her pal from school, Susan Ryan. Susan had taken her through all the introductory paces last fall. Real sweet kid. Very droll.

On the way home, we neared Dick "Mac" Ryan's house. I told Kate I'd bring her up to see the mare and foal.

Susan piped up, "My grand uncle has a mare and foal here also."

I turned around and said, "Is Dick Ryan your uncle?"

"Yes."

Another loop closed.

Thursday, June 6. Intellectually, today was my first really lazy day in quite some time. My formal schedule is over, although I might still do a Business College lecture next week, time permitting. It was nice to know I didn't have a paper hanging over my head.

I started hoeing out and packing stuff in my office, but otherwise it was a quiet day.

Mary and I went in to the Thursday Church/State program in the evening.

Friday, June 7. I spent the morning writing and paying bills. We're sinking into debt, but it seems worth it. It has been a tremendous year for all of us.

Later in the day, Mary joined me at the Stables and we learned that both Eoin O'Sullivan and John Coakley had birthdays coming up soon. We wouldn't be here for the actual birthdays but the occasions would provide an excuse and a vehicle for a great party. We decided, on the spot, to put something together.

The three of us had a late dinner home and then headed in different directions. Kate was off to the Annacotty Youth Center disco (well chaperoned, I might add), Mary went over to Niamh O'Sullivan's for "tea and bickies," and I took some photos of the stud farm up to Alan O'Reilly at Finnegan's. They were the pictures I had promised to send to "Tiny."

While I was standing there, a fellow I had never seen before, who had heard my Yankee voice, announced that he was from Los Angeles. His name was, hang on, Tom Cruse. He had just arrived in Limerick that day to work for the Molex Corporation at Shannon Development. His family was following in a month or so. Didn't know a soul. I felt like I'd come full circle. I was now the old pro telling the newcomer about the subculture of Ireland.

Saturday, June 8. Our old friends from Syracuse, Diane and Fred Murphy, their kids, and Diane's mother were scheduled to arrive today. We were really looking forward to their visit. We've only talked with a handful of Americans since we've been here.

It was pouring when we picked them up. Not a very auspicious welcome to Ireland, but certainly a traditional one.

Sunday, June 9. We all trooped down the road to the 11:00 Mass at Ahane.

Fr. Minogue was in rare form, although he was mercifully short. The sermon was on the presence of the devil (which he saw everywhere). Then he launched into a brief but vigorous dissertation on rock music, drugs, Black Masses and Satan worship—all in the United States. God forbid that such things ever happen in Holy Catholic Ireland! I got the distinct impression that this stuff was going on all over America and I had obviously been living in a vacuum. The Murphys were stunned. They had everything they could do to contain themselves.

Fred particularly was taken with the Bachelors' Row at the back of the church. Said it reminded him of his farm family in Pennsylvania.

After Mass, we went for a spin down a one-lane country road. They all loved it. It was only five minutes from our house but fifty years away.

Fred and Diane drove me in to Ryan's for the papers. They got a great kick out of the store, especially the loaves of brown bread sitting unwrapped on the shelf.

We headed off to Loch Gur and the Neolithic ruins southwest of Limerick City. Mary had packed a nice picnic lunch for the whole gang. Our first stop was the Grange Circle, one of several stone circles about four thousand years old that apparently had cultural, astronomic, and religious dimensions to them. The circle was formed by huge chunks of limestone (several tons heft), two of which are slabs so constructed as to form a solar V during the summer solstice. One can only speculate on the exact nature of the formation.

We then drove around to the main grounds of the ancient encampment. It included replicated houses, a museum with Stone, Bronze, and Iron Age instruments and weapons, more stone circles, a Mesolithic tomb (for the tribal chiefs) and some castle ruins from a later period.

Monday, June 10. Mary and Kate were off to the Dublin Zoo this morning. They were taking a number of kids from the Limerick ghettoes up on the train. The Murphys went sightseeing and I left for the dedication of the Foundation Building at the University.

The laying of the Foundation stone drew a fairly impressive crowd.

The guest list brought out most of the university and city establishment, and the program participants represented a pretty good cross-section of the "power structure": the Ministers for Commerce and Education, the American Ambassador, Dick Moore, a few of the Irish Plutocracy, Liz Shannon, widow of former Ambassador Bill Shannon, and Jim O'Connor, an American multimillionaire from Manhasset, New York, who is Chairman of the Foundation.

Right before the ceremony began, the Irish Defense Forces Band played the "Star Spangled Banner." It was the first time I'd heard it since we left home. While I don't like the anthem as a song (I prefer "America the Beautiful")—it sure raised a lump in my throat.

During the course of the day I must have met several dozen people with whom I shared some mutual friends. The compactness and intimacy of Ireland was brought home rather forcefully as I began to realize the numbers of people who knew each other throughout this small country. I think I now understand why there are so few scandals. For a scandal to occur, a secret has to be unearthed, and everybody here already knows everything! Someone suggested that if Watergate had taken place in Ireland, Nixon would have remained in office, but everyone in the entire country would have known who "Deep Throat" was.

Tuesday, June 11. Fr. Mick Molloy called from Archbishop Cassidy's office in Tuam. When were we coming up? We decided to go tomorrow.

During the course of the day, a very savvy young business student of mine, Sean O'Toole, came by the office. He is leaving soon for a job in New York and wanted some pointers. We talked at some length and then I managed to turn the conversation to my favorite subject—the sociology of the Irish culture. We touched on the Church and I gathered that while he is rather skeptical, he is nonetheless a regular participant. He told me one story about his parish priest standing in the pulpit and denouncing a parishioner by name. That made Fr. Minogue's lectures on genuflecting and the sign of the cross—or even sex and money—sound pretty tame. Sean said it was fairly common practice when he was younger. The priests ruled through raw fear—particularly in country villages such as his.

It was ironic that before I left the house this morning I was listening to Radio Clare and they played "The Ballad of Eamon Casey." Casey is the Bishop of Galway, a popular liberal who verbally fought against U.S. policy in Central America, who boycotted Ronald Reagan when he received an honorary Doctorate from University College, Galway, and who has managed to rack up several new Mercedes while apparently under the weather.

The "Ballad," of course, recounts all those episodes. I found the two extremes—the screaming parish priest and the tippling prelate—fascinating.

Wednesday, June 12. The Murphy clan left for Cork City, West Cork, and the Ring of Kerry, and we went north to Tuam, the west coast of County Mayo and Galway.

The weather was pleasant on the way north, although the wind blew in savagely off the ocean and actually swayed the car several times.

We only got half-lost in Tuam, a seemingly bustling town located a few miles northeast of Galway City. Finally found the Cathedral by following the spire. The Presbytery (and Diocesan office) is actually out behind the church. The Cathedral itself is neo-Gothic, built in 1832, with Tudor or Norman turrets (I've always had trouble distinguishing). The manse is an Edwardian gem from 1905, special-built for the Bishop.

Fr. Mick Molloy, who is Secretary of the Diocese, met us in the office. A delightful, chunky man of forty-three, with flecked gray hair, he was wearing sandals at the time. He had a great smile and a ruddy complexion. I could tell he was as anxious to meet us, as we were to see him. He couldn't have been more gracious.

Kate really didn't want any part of the program until he started producing items from the archives, e.g., a gold chalice and paten from around 1640.

Many priests had had to flee Ireland during the Repression and they left their church possessions in safekeeping with Galway Catholics. Some were returned and ended up in the diocesan archives, some disappeared, and one chalice showed up in Spain three hundred years later.

Fr. Mick had overdone himself on the biography of Bishop Gilmartin, Congresswoman Kelly's great uncle. He had tons of material and newspaper articles. We even went into the safe and took a picture of the Bishop's pectoral cross. We toured the slowly growing library and the main refectory with its original Chippendale furniture and Waterford crystalware. The Presbytery serves as both a home for Archbishop Cassidy and as the diocesan offices, the chancery.

After viewing the art collection, et. al., we drove over to the Cre na Cille Restaurant. The name literally means "the land near the cemetery." The cemetery was across the street. There we had a magnificent but simple lunch and a simply magnificent conversation.

We talked about the See of Tuam (established I think in the fourth or fifth century by St. Jarlath, Patron of the Diocese). Diocesan records go back to the twelfth century!

Fr. Molloy was raised on a farm. When he was ordained in 1974, the Bishop assigned him to the Aran Islands, out beyond the mouth of Galway Bay. No electricity. No amenities. The locals all spoke Irish. There was not even a store on the Islands. Provisions were brought in by boat or on an occasional plane. The natives fished for the most part, although he said there was some farming and herding. The biggest social event was the Station Mass where the priest would travel from place to place, island to island, celebrating Masses in homes. Then the "creature" was broken out and a party ensued. He said he even found a piano somewhere and had it shipped out.

Several items in his portrayal intrigued me. He said the fishermen never carried life preservers in their curraghs (the long, swift native fishing boats)—only Holy Water. They never swam in the ocean. The water was there to provide them sustenance. It was not to be used (or perhaps abused) for pleasure. He said he had some frightening experiences in the curraghs where they were actually bailing out as they rowed against ferocious waves and swells. He told about one funeral where the removal was from the mainland by curragh, and the mourners caravanned by boat through a storm. Strangely enough, he noted that they didn't bury their dead at sea. They buried them either in raised graves or in sandy tracts—the land was too rocky to dig graves—and always wrapped the coffin in a white cloth to preserve some dignity. It was a riveting monologue.

At that point, we launched off to a discussion of John Millington Synge's *Riders of the Sea*.

After a quick tour of the Cathedral and some ritual photographs, we continued northwest through Castlebar and Westport in Mayo.

The drive to Westport was beautiful. Because of the sinuous path of the road, the mountains seemingly loomed up on all four sides of us. I noticed that the neat, measured stone walls that fenced in the fields of Clare and Galway had almost disappeared. We were in Mayo—God help us—an anarchic area if ever there was one. Any walls or fences would have been out of place.

Once through the harbor town of Westport, we took the coast road along beside Clew Bay. As we headed toward the ocean, the water took on a sea-green cast. The road wound between the shoreline and a ridge of escarpments, and the contrast was striking.

As we came into the little village of Louisburg, we stopped to get our bearings. It was a town at the end of the earth. One intersection with no traffic. Hardly any cars around. Two pedestrians, one barely mobile. The place was dead. Then I recalled something Mick Molloy had said about the West of Mayo. Industry was gone and the area had many, many "dead villages." They all looked neat and clean, with nice rows of cottages. On closer inspection, however, one found that the houses actually had been closed up and locked. In a word, deserted. Louisburg was not technically deserted, but it appeared to be on its last legs. It was incredible, since the place is only a stone's throw from the ocean. I couldn't help thinking that people in New York, New Jersey, or Southern California would kill for shore space like this.

I had seen a sign for Roonah Quay and Roonah Pier and I was determined to find them before the sun went down. We drove for about six miles off the beaten path through stone fields. God, it was desolate—like a scene from *Playboy of the Western World*. Every now and then a small modern house would pop up in the distance, but it was raw and bleak country. Everything West Mayo was supposed to be. Even the sheep and cows grazed unfettered by falling walls or disheveled hedgerows. They roved in the fields and along the edges of the road. It was as though the animals had plagiarized the anarchy and independence of their nominal owners.

We rolled over a hillock and, presto, there before us lay the majestic Atlantic, as ruthless and powerful as could be. The tide was coming in and the water lashed at the craggy shoreline. Ten-feet swells were followed by thirty-feet surges of surf. It was spectacular and awesome.

We stood for several minutes in the wild ocean spray and squinted at Clare Island about four to five miles offshore. There was a mist hanging over the island, although the sun was bright where we were. Roonah Pier is the ferry point for the island taxi.

Heading south through the mountains, it soon became apparent we were moving into a glen of some sort. We didn't have a clue what to expect. What we found was beyond our wildest dreams. We were on the Dhulloch Pass road, which, unlike the Conor Pass on Dingle, went along the base of the mountains. It was a time warp. It was prehistoric. Nothing had been changed by man and not too much, probably, had been changed naturally in centuries. It was breathtaking, with dozens of waterfalls cascading down the mountainsides, forming beautiful lochs right beside the road. There were hundreds of sheep roaming all over. Many had paint-marks daubed on their backs, which was the only indication of human presence. We never saw another soul.

The regal power of the mountains juxtaposed with the serenity of the lakes and the passivity of the sheep was like alternate shots of adrenalin and a sedative.

And so it went for the better part of thirty miles, until we reached Killary Harbour and Leenane.

For the next hour, we wound through the Maamtuck and Connemara Mountains. It was an equally spectacular part of the journey, but the mountains were more fearsome and the roads more serpentine. By then, the three of us were a little overdosed on beauty. It was close to 7:00.

We stopped in a motel outside Galway City, and after eating and getting settled, I walked down to the pub to catch the local flavor. I chatted with a fellow whose name, coincidentally, was Molloy. He was a good friend of my young colleague at the University, Eoin O'Sullivan. They had grown up together in Galway. Another loop closed.

Thursday, June 13. This morning, we drove over to take a reminiscent picture in front of St. Oliver Plunkett Church. Plunkett was a Catholic Bishop from Drogheda who had been martyred during the Repression. Six years ago, Mary, Kate, my mother, and I had gone to this church for Easter Sunday Mass. The parish had festooned the church with wild-colored banners. It had looked like a medieval joust.

Mom was not quite "clicking" that morning and said soberly and seriously, "This must be a Ukrainian church."

Mary and I laughed out loud that day, and we laughed again today remembering it. It's now part of our family lore.

We meandered down the Dock Road, through the old wharf section, and over to Claddagh. Claddagh, of course, is the area enshrined in the song "Galway Bay," and known throughout the world for the Claddagh Rings. It was an ancient fishing village alongside the Norse port of Galway, but it was Irish-speaking, independent, and had its own king. Until about sixty years ago, the entire waterfront was full of thatched cottages. It is still comprised mostly of working class Galwegians and there are many fishing trawlers around the piers where the River Corrib flows into Galway Bay. But its old identity has pretty well disappeared.

The Beach Road around the edge of Claddagh continued for several miles.

The next area, and the end of our trek toward the west, was Salt Hill, a trendy, fairly modern, resort town.

At a quick glance, Salt Hill looks like Rehoboth Beach, Delaware, or almost any other ocean beach town. Closer scrutiny, however, reveals that the beach is rocky and the strand is concrete. Wood is too expensive to build a boardwalk, and sand is a rare commodity indeed in Ireland.

We headed back through the non-beach Salt Hill, over to University College, Galway, and the Cathedral.

UCG is not a particularly attractive campus. The original building and quadrangle adornments are fairly classical Victorian limestone. The rest of the place looks like University College, Dublin—slab stone buildings with lots of windows. Aesthetically blah. Strictly government issue.

The River Corrib flows past the University (several rowing clubs are located in the backwater), then around the Cathedral, which is an awesome Romanesque structure. Mary commented that it looked like a shrine.

The Church is called the Cathedral of Mary Being Assumed Into Heaven On St. Nicholas—a real mouthful. It is constructed of native granite, and the floor of the interior is cut of multi-hued Connemara marble. Exquisitely crafted, but stark.

We drove back through Tipperary. It had been a great trip.

Friday, June 14. A number of my students stopped by the office this morning. One needed a sponsor to get to San Francisco, which I was able to arrange with a couple of phone calls. Another wanted some help with a job in Germany. Fortunately, I was able to assist there as well. Ciaran Fahy, a Business major, dropped in for a visit. Unknown to me, he was from Tuam and knew Fr. Mick Molloy very well. Another loop tied up. He was not, however, aware of the fabulous diocesan collection. He plans to go up to see it in a couple of weeks.

I picked Mary up and we went out to Glenstal Abbey for lunch with our Benedictine monk friend, Henry O'Shea. He's a marvelous host and conversationalist. Brian Murphy, another monk, popped into the little private dining room where were eating. He is a brilliant historian. He had just published "Patrick Pearse and the Lost Republican Ideal." It put a decidedly republican slant on the Irish State since the partition of the island. He had been working on the book when we first met at David and Eva Coombes' house over the Christmas holidays.

Brian is a very handsome man, probably sixty, with finely chiseled features, full white hair, and rosy cheeks.

We had a delightful chat about the book, his research sources, and the fact that he was now probably under surveillance by the Garda.

"Were it not for his impeccable intellectual credentials (an A.B. from Oxford, a PhD. from University College, Dublin, an STD. from Maynooth), he would be looked upon as a republican bomb thrower," Henry mused.

We all chuckled nervously. He autographed a copy of the book for Mary and me, and asked if I would deliver an autographed copy to our mutual hero, Speaker Tip O'Neill, when I got back to the States.

Henry O'Shea was raised in upscale circumstances. His father is a physician, an Irish Army medical officer. During lunch, we discussed the question of a widening economic and social cleavage in Irish society, with the rich getting filthy rich, the middle class just surviving, and the really poor fast becoming a huge majority of the population. I mentioned Alan O'Reilly's comments at Finnegan's about the prospects of an upheaval from the left, and Henry agreed.

He pointed out the wealth at Glenstal Abbey school, hitherto pretty much unknown—students flown back and forth from home in helicopters, kids whisked away by their parents for a weekend in the Bahamas—while kids in South Hill, Moyross and other slums don't even know where their next meal is coming from, in spite of the dole. It was a fairly vivid portrayal of the roots of a new civil war.

After lunch, Henry took us into a catacomb/mini-museum beneath the Abbey church. A collection of about thirty Russian icons from the sixteenth and seventeenth centuries was housed there.

My mouth dropped open. I actually made myself touch several of them. They were splendid in color, in artistry, and with some, in silversmithery. The collection had been given to the Abbey about forty years ago, but mostly gathered dust until recently. The pieces were taken to the National Gallery in Dublin, cleaned, and returned a couple of years ago. They now repose in this little sanctuary.

The lighting scheme was unique. The small electric bulbs were covered almost two thirds by metal brackets and spaced about two inches away from the icons. This gave the effect of tapers, thus enhancing the mystery and mood of the Orthodox mentality. It was a tremendous show.

Saturday, June 15. Kate took the Murphys with her up to Ashroe, and in the afternoon, their whole clan left for the Burren. We loafed around and eventually went over to John and Margaret Stapleton's for a cookout. Nice quiet day.

Sunday, June 16. The Murphys all went out to Glenstal Abbey for early Mass, Kate joined her crew at Ahane, and Mary and I planned to go in to the Jesuit church in the afternoon. About mid-morning, the clan returned and announced that although they'd already been to Mass, they were going back to the Latin Mass at noon. We decided to go with them.

The Mass was a special occasion. It was the Profession of Final Vows for one of the brothers. (Some of the monks are ordained priests; others become brothers.) What an event! The entire community of monks processed into the church. It was an old-time Latin High Mass, complete with the choir (including Henry O'Shea) leading, and all the monks responding. The procession itself was beautiful. Dom Celestine Cullen, the Abbot, read a dissertation on obedience in the monastic life. The community chanted the ancient Litany of the Saints in Latin– "Sancti Johanni, ora pro nobis," etc. The elder Murphys hadn't seen anything like this in twenty-five years—since Vatican II—and the kids had NEVER seen anything like it.

The Brother then signed the Profession on the altar and went from monk to monk showing each his signed commitment. It was very moving.

There were half a dozen prayers chanted in Latin, including the "Gloria." The ceremony was not only replete with ancient rhythms, it was pregnant with poignancy. It was as though time had stood still and the Abbey had been snatched away, temporarily, from the clutches of the earth. The incense, the Gregorian composition, the simple solemnity, the sense of timeless obligation and timely application, all combined to produce a feeling of the preternatural.

Monday, June 17. Today was a wrap-up-the-loose-ends-day around the office.

Just before dinner, I ran up to Finnegan's to take a couple of snapshots for the album. I figured the place would be quiet at that hour, but that I might at least catch Tom Berkery. He was there with a pleasantly disheveled friend, Johnny Rainsford. Johnny looked like a caricature of every country Irishman—blurry-eyed, ruddily complected, gaunt, with windstrewn hair and a trench coat of ancient vintage. I caught the two of them at the bar—with their pints of Guinness. It was a photographer's dream.

About 9:30, Fred, Diane, Mary and I drove in to Nancy Blake's Pub in town. One of my students had suggested we stop in on a Monday night a little before 10:00 to hear some traditional Irish music. The timing was perfect. We got the last four stools in the place.

Blake's is an intimate little pub tucked away on a side street in downtown Limerick. There were no signs of life from the outside, but it was booming inside. Mostly twenty-five to thirty-year-olds (with the exception of the musicians, who were all students at the University).

True to form, the place filled up about 10:30. There were four kids playing—a young lady who worked an excellent fiddle, a fellow who played the guitar but could make it sound like a mandolin, a banjoist who doubled on the tin whistle, and my student, Nollaig (Noel) Scott, who played a virtuoso concertina. Another lad vocalized with the guitar. The only instrument missing was the bodhran, the traditional Irish hand drum. They played for almost two hours without a break. Sang ditties and parodies as well. It was great "craic." The crowd loved it, and the musicians obviously loved doing it.

Nancy Blake came over when she heard Mary and Diane chatting between numbers. She wondered where they were from. When Diane responded "Syracuse," her eyes lit up.

"My daughter and son-in-law live right outside Syracuse," she said.

To top it off, she told us her daughter was studying at Syracuse University—in Diane's Department (Diane is Director of Women's Studies). The loops, even the international loops, continue to get smaller in Ireland.

At closing time, the crowd headed out the door and dissipated. Within two minutes, people had disappeared into alleys and side streets. Ours was the only car on the street. A dead silence fell over the neighborhood. *Brigadoon* and *Germelshausern* had been swallowed up again. Another part of the mysterious charm of this country.

Tuesday, June 18. The Murphys left for Galway in the morning. I felt flu-like but went in to school to do some calling, faxing, and visiting. I was so sore and exhausted by three o'clock, however, that I went home. It was a very unproductive day.

Wednesday, June 19. I drove out to John Wrenn's house in Fedamore this morning to negotiate the repurchase of the car he had sold me last fall. John and his wife Margaret are lovely, meticulous people, just scraping together a living. He told me the tax officials are constantly after him, a complaint I've heard from Liam O'Shea, Pat McGrath, and a host of other middle-class entrepreneurs. He said that between the taxes and the money he had tied up in other cars, he was not in a position to buy the car back from me.

My stomach started to knot up, with only ten days to go before departure. He told me he thought he could find a buyer, however, and would be back to me soon.

I asked him for an estimate on the car, and he replied, "Six hundred to seven hundred pounds."

I tried to act nonchalant and said that was the area I had in mind. Actually, I was thrilled. It meant I'd been able to drive for about sixty or seventy dollars a month since last September. Admittedly, the car was not a Jaguar XJ6, but it had run, and we covered a lot of miles in it.

When I got back to school, Anne McCarthy from the department office asked me if I was going to be around at 4:30 on Monday.

I said I probably would, and she responded, "Oh good, because that's when your going away party is!"

It reminded me of the surprise fiftieth birthday party Mary threw for me and then forgot to invite me.

I had lunch at the University Club with a most engaging and interesting man, Mr. Tom O'Donnell, a former member of the Dail. I was amazed at our parallel careers and consanguinity of interests. He went into politics early in life, had a successful and fun career, and decided to get out of it and spend more time with his family. He's perhaps six or seven years older than I am, and he now lectures at the University and Chairs the Irish Peace Institute, which is located on campus.

Tom was a Fine Gael Deputy from East Limerick and a very close friend of Brian Lenihan. He was Shadow Transport Minister when Brian carried the Portfolio, and vice versa. He also served a stint as a Member of the European Parliament and specialized in transportation and regionalism. He was very excited about my American Studies proposal because of the relevance it has to the emerging European Community—particularly the American experience with federalism. He offered whatever assistance and influence he could bring to bear.

Tom gave me my first real insight into why Ireland instituted a proportional representation system in the Dail: first, because the British didn't have one and the Irish wanted to be different, and second, because they wanted to preserve a multiplicity of parties. He pointed out that in one election in England, the Liberals had gotten twenty percent of the popular vote, but only one seat in the House of Commons. The Irish thought such a system inherently unfair and so opted for proportional representation. For all its shortcomings, real or imagined, a coalition government is considered better than a squeeze on minority parties.

I stopped over at the Stables on the way home and several students approached me. Some were graduating; others were underclassmen. The came individually to tell me how much they had enjoyed my lectures, and how appreciative they were for the personal interest I had taken in them and their course work.

They were all hopeful that a full-time arrangement could be worked out for the American Studies program this coming fall, because it had such great value for the University. These conversations made me feel as good as anything that has happened here all year.

I walked up to Finnegan's about 10:30 to catch the latest news. One of the "hot potatoes" in the neighborhood is the new halting site for the Travelers. They've just been driven away from the gates of the University and the front of the elegant new Castletroy Park Hotel. The County Council bought a prime piece of land for them on the Dublin Road (reputedly, for about a half million dollars). They purchased it from a local car dealer. According to the pub gossip, the dealer had been trying to develop the property, but couldn't get council permission for access from the main road. He also didn't have water or electricity. The council bought the land, gave him an option to buy it back in two years, opened the access road permanently and brought in water and power. I don't think anyone will be surprised if two years from now the land is developed into one-acre lots for a housing estate. It's Democracy in Action!

Thursday, June 20. I found it hard to accept the fact this morning that we only have one week left on this journey. It has been a long, sometimes difficult year, with a distinct decline in our material living standards, and a number of emotional sacrifices as well. The pluses have so far outstripped the minuses, however, as to be absolutely disproportionate.

Mary drove me in to the bank, and somehow I managed to stitch together some money for the party tomorrow night. I'm a little surprised at the level of excitement I've detected among the invitees. Apparently house parties are not that common because of the size of most homes and because of the pub culture, so there is an air of novelty to our gathering. We're anticipating a great evening.

Friday, January 21. I drove over to the post office and re-directed our mail for the duration. It cost me fifteen pounds.

The postmistress clipped the cash to the form and said, "I'll send this in to Limerick."

I never questioned the arrangement. That's how comfortable I feel with the level of ethical conduct here. Many times at the bank, I've noticed piles of tens and twenties sitting on the counter within reach of anyone (there are no cages or bars—that would be impersonal). The money is never touched, and as far as I have observed, never even watched.

That afternoon, one of the crazier episodes of the year began. We were going to need lots of ice cubes for the party, and the fridge only held about four trays. I assumed I could pick up a couple of fifty-pound bags at the supermarket or in one of the small convenience shops. Wrong. There are no such things as bags of ice cubes in Limerick—or probably in Ireland, for that matter. They simply don't have them. First, it's part of the culture not to have large house/dinner parties, so there isn't the need for a quantity of cubes. Second, most people drink stout, lager, or wine and they don't have to be refrigerator-chilled. "Cool" is cold enough for the average person here. Whisky drinkers prefer their drinks "neat."

Despite what I realized would be a relatively small demand, I believed there had to be a supply somewhere and so I went after it. I must have made ten phone calls to different stores and service stations. The response was universal. "Why would we carry such an item?" I even checked the Yellow Pages under Ice Machines (there was obviously nothing listed under Ice). I thought maybe somebody could tell me of a place that had purchased a cube maker. No luck. It was suggested that I try my "local" or perhaps the Limerick Inn. The Limerick Inn was probably the best bet because of the volume of tourists.

After almost an hour on the phone, I called Finnegan's. Sure, they'd be happy to help with whatever I needed. As a backup, I also called the Stables bar. The bartender said he'd have a bag as well.

The house looked great when I got home. Mary had colored ribbons hanging everywhere, hundreds of buttercups, which Kate had picked in the fields, a beautiful birthday cake, and enough food for an army. I don't know how she does it. She's fantastic. The neighbors, of course, had pitched in and loaned us china, silver, glasses, an electric knife, etc.

About 8:00 I went to Finnegan's to pick up the ice. The bartender gave me a plastic trash bag full of cubes. I felt obligated to go into the Stables. I was met at the door with a bag about the size of a lady's purse. The ice machine was on the "fritz." Oh well, one out of two is pretty good in Ireland!

We had suggested a nine o'clock (or later) schedule, so we really had no idea when people would arrive. A caravan (which had first rendezvoused at the Black Swan in Annacotty) arrived a little after 9:00 with about a dozen people.

It was a slow starter, with people clustered in small groups talking quietly. I was afraid that if the rest of the crowd didn't show, those who were there would be overwhelmed by the size of the house. A little past ten, more arrived and we started to put the food out.

By then the gang had warmed up. When I heard the first giddy laugh, I knew we were getting off the ground.

There was a steady flow for the next hour or so, and about midnight several troops from Dublin, including the two honorees, showed up. The party was in full bloom and there was a pronounced din in the house.

Around 1:00, Brian Faloon began doing some Russian folk dances in the den and the show really began to move. (Faloon also treated us to a series of East European folk songs.) There were Irish ballads, and yours truly sang Jolson and Americana.

The 747 that had taken a couple of hours to rev up was now airborne and the flight lasted for another three hours.

By 4:00, most of the crowd had departed. It was comical. We had partied through the darkness of the summer night. (11:00 p.m. to 4:00 a.m.). It was as light out when people left as when they had come.

It had been a magnificent party with almost all the gang who had become my "University family" during the year. All in all, between thirty and forty people had shown.

Saturday, June 22. This was an obviously short day. No one even surfaced until 1:00 in the afternoon. We cleaned up without too much trouble. It had not been a raucous party, just fun, and so except for the odd wine glass stuck in a seat cushion or under a table, the place was not in bad shape. We did a postmortem and the "day after" was almost as much fun as the "evening of."

The Murphys returned that night.

Sunday, June 23. We drove out to Shannon Airport with the Murphys very early in the morning.

We arrived at Shannon a little after 7:00, but could find no check-in gate. They were on a charter, leaving at 9:40, so I reckoned they would be using a scheduled airline gate—probably Aer Lingus. They were, but we were told it wouldn't open for two more hours. I felt that was cutting it short for loading a transatlantic flight. Found a monitor. Their plane wasn't due to arrive until 10:50 with a 12:20 departure. Diane checked the tickets, then turned beet red. They were supposed to be there for check-in at 9:40, not departure, which meant there was now a five-hour wait.

Since we were ahead of schedule, the kids went scouting, Fred and I went into the Burren Lounge for a cup of coffee, and the ladies went to the duty-free shop. I asked Diane's mother if she had any money to exchange.

"I did," she said, "but I got in there and decided to spend it instead."

I commented on the female logic of it all—to her delight.

After the Murphy's departed, we headed back to Mass at Ahane. Fr. Minogue was like a rambling rose. Pat O'Sullivan, with classic Irish understatement, said on the way out, "He does go on, doesn't he?"

Mary wanted to make one last pilgrimage to the cousins in Newmarket-on-Fergus and Lissycasey, so we packed a picnic lunch and left about mid-afternoon.

While we were having tea at the Ryans', Kate and her traveling mate, Charlene Bridgeman, seemed to have disappeared. We still had to drive all the way to West Clare and I wanted to make this stop respectably short. They weren't around the house, so I went up into the fields looking for them.

I had to cross two pastures, and when I called the girls, I heard a rustling behind me. There were about fifteen two-ton bull cattle coming toward me at a trot. I froze. Didn't understand enough about them to know what they'd do. I'd never heard of cattle turning on anyone, but they surrounded me, all drooling and moon-eyed.

I thought, "Ye Gods, I'm about to be lynched by a bunch of drug-crazed cows!"

Where the hell was Gary Larson when I needed him!

I managed to screw up enough courage to flail my arms and shout at them. They all scattered and I felt suddenly very powerful. As I walked on toward the next pasture, however, they all fell into pattern and followed me—menacingly. Now I began to think they'd just been leading me on.

"They're going to get me out in the middle of the far pastures, where no one can hear me, and trample me to death," I rationalized.

One spotted black and white actually started to run toward me. I swung my arms and he shied away.

I called the girls several times, with the animals all staring at me. No response. When I headed back toward the house, the cattle again began to follow. I walked faster. So did they. By the time I made it up the last boreen and through the gate, they were all right on my tail. One of them was nuzzling the gate as I shut it.

It had been such a crazy experience, and I felt so stupid, that I never mentioned it to anyone.

We reached Lissycasey around seven o'clock and caught them all by surprise, which was our intention. The whole tribe was there.

For an eighty-five-year-old, Patrick was as perky as could be. His memory is fantastic. He told us all about the family, which ones went to America, which didn't. We had never even heard the names of some of Mary's grandmother's siblings. As we talked about Mary's grandmother, Bridget suggested we might want to make a quick visit to the church where she had worshipped as a child. We did, and it was a special treat for Mary.

Monday, June 24. During an otherwise funny reprise of last Friday's party, one sour note was heard. Paul McCutcheon hadn't been personally invited, and didn't show up. I felt terrible. Paul had been like family all year. It's an interesting feature of the Irish culture. No one would think of going to someone's house or party without a specific invitation—unlike the States where herd movements, particularly among the groupy barroom set, are commonplace. A loosely made invitation simply won't do for many people here.

I had a meeting on American Studies with Dean Paddy Doran early in the afternoon. He was so laid back, funny and talkative I could hardly believe my ears. We went up and down the Irish culture, Irish politics, literature, families, academia. At one point he told me a story about someone he knew in Ireland who had risen from humble origins to great prominence, and then proceeded to forget his roots.

"He acted as though he didn't have an arse in his pants," said Paddy, with obvious relish.

He was very apologetic about his relationship with me. Felt he had left me in the lurch and that I'd been bored stiff. I think he was actually shocked to learn how busy I had been and how heavy a teaching load I had carried. I enjoyed the conversation. It was a side of him I had not seen. He was very perceptive, terribly overworked and slightly cynical —but not the potty professor of my earlier imagination. He promised to be more attentive to the development of American Studies.

Mary came in later to join me at the wine and cheese departure ceremony Henry Ellis had organized. They presented me with an autographed hardback copy of the Hunt Museum Book. The Hunt Museum, which is housed in the University, has one of the finest collections of Bronze and Stone Age relics, and ancient silver, gold, and gem decorative pieces in Ireland, perhaps in Europe.

Mary and I stopped over to visit a couple we'd been meaning to call on for months, Joe and Phil McNamara. Phil is a docent at the Hunt Museum and a thoroughly delightful lady. Joe is a semi-retired accountant. They are impeccably correct and articulate, as only the well-educated Irish can be, and forthright as well. He speaks an Anglo-Irish which almost sounds affected, but isn't. I would imagine they are in their late sixties or early seventies.

Joe was wearing a blue satin paisley smoking robe when we arrived, and ceremoniously escorted us to our seats in the living room. The conversation was very cordial, but equally formal. He is almost fastidious in his language. The topics of discussion ranged all over the lot, but the two recurrent themes were Irish history and an analysis of the Irish Character.

These are almost demonically repetitive subjects among the Irish. In this case, neither Joe nor Phil appeared to have much use for the Irish hoi polloi.

As we walked to the dining room for tea, it struck me who Joe reminded me of. With his ample girth, elegant robe, slicked down hair parted at the center, and horn-rimmed glasses with Coke-bottle lenses, he was Ernie Kovacs without the moustache. Kovacs wrote and starred in an outrageously funny vignette on television thirty-five-years-ago called "Outside the Bookends," with Percy Dovetonsils as the poet-protagonist. Joe was a dead-ringer. I had to stifle my thoughts, lest I laugh out loud.

Tuesday, June 25. I drove in to Villiers to pick up Kate's grades early this morning. She made honors in everything but math. She was first in her class in history. Not too shabby for an uprooted kid!

Spent the rest of the morning on the phone drumming up moral and financial support for American Studies. Called almost anyone I could find—either in Ireland or in the States.

Mary and Kate both had engagements in the evening, and I planned a quiet period at home. I was reading when the doorbell rang. It was Patti Punch with Henry O'Shea, in his monk's robe. He had wanted to come over to say good-bye last Friday, but the community was put on special retreat for the weekend and he couldn't get away. Patti agreed to pick him up tonight and see if we were home.

I managed to scrape up some chilled wine for them, and when that was gone and there was nothing else left in the house, I suggested we go up to Finnegan's. Henry flipped off the robe in two seconds. He had on a green street shirt, slacks and loafers underneath.

"Let's go," he said.

We stood and talked at Finnegan's until almost midnight.

Wednesday, June 25. John Coakley and I met this morning with Dr. Angela Chambers, who chairs one of the departments in the College of Humanities. Angela has endorsed the idea of an American Studies Center and feels the machinery is already in place to implement it. They could appoint me Director in September, but it would still require outside funding. In other words, ""John, we'll give you the academic and research vehicle, the physical plant, and faculty backup. You come up with the money." I had already inferred that funding would be my obligation, but Angela's endorsement and John's verbal support were critical ingredients.

Ambassador Moore faxed me from Dublin this afternoon. He is very supportive of my American Studies initiative. Asked me to come up to the Embassy to meet with him when we return in September.

By evening, the nightmare of our departure was beginning to sink into our consciousness. Only thirty-six-hours till we embarked and the house was still in shambles. We had so many family, social, and professional obligations to fulfill that we were probably two days behind schedule already. Because everything is so personal in Ireland, we took time to see as many people as possible and to convey an air of nonchalance. The sub-surface stress level, of course, was almost unbelievable.

Where are those beach sneakers? Did they get thrown out or are they in Box #6? Has anybody seen my green sweater? Is the Dawn Dairy bill paid? Who's going to help us cart this stuff to the airport? Where's the little black phone number book? My God, the guy hasn't even shown up with the renewal contract on the house! We need labels for the luggage and rope for the book boxes. Kate, you can't just throw everything into boxes. You have to sort that junk out! To hell with John Wrenn. I'm just going to leave the goddamn car in the driveway and hope somebody steals it. It's worth more in insurance than it is in a resale anyway. Mom, Charlene and Yvonne want to stay overnight. Can they? Where the hell are you going? Up to Finnegan's? Just great!

I walked into Finnegan's and Paul McC utcheon and Jim Deegan were at the bar. They are a neat pair, bright and sassy. Paul, who is in his early thirties, is already a highly published lawyer-lecturer, and Deegan, who is thirtyish, is a street-smart economist working on his doctorate. Neither had made the party last week and wanted to have a good-bye drink. They are both delightful cynics—in a uniquely Irish way.

We were in an animated conversation when Coakley, O'Sullivan, Rees and Eugene Gath (a brilliant mathmetician who did his Doctorate at MIT) walked in. They had all gotten me out under false pretenses.

We repaired to a table—a rare departure in a pub— where Paul presented me, on behalf of all those desperadoes, a copy of Charles Sullivan's "Ireland in Poetry." I was flabbergasted. They knew how poignant a gift it was—that I loved Ireland and poetry. (Mary had given me Sullivan's "America in Poetry" a couple of years ago.) It was a most warm gesture.

Having approached the emotional border, they then reverted to type.

Deegan said, "Is the owner a fascist?"

This was a code. It meant simply: will this guy throw us out at closing time, or is he civilized? I told them it depended on his mood and he appeared to be in good humor tonight.

I left a little after midnight, and the boys were still enjoying themselves. I went home to learn that Mary had agreed to let Kate have a party tomorrow afternoon for her gang in the neighborhood. I suppose we should both be put in a rubber room, but we felt it was important for her to satisfy HER social obligations as well.

Thursday, June 27. We arose early, knowing full well that today was only going to be about half as long as we needed—at best.

We sorted out our schedules, appointments, necessary phone calls, etc., and then proceeded, ant-like, to carry out the chores.

Mary treated Niamh O'Sullivan, Dierdre O'Sullivan, and Martha Laffan to an elegant lunch at the University Club. She couldn't have made it this year without them. I made the rounds of the secretaries and staff to do my au revoirs.

We came home late in the afternoon to fifteen or twenty kids in the house for Kate's going-away party. They had converted the living room into a restaurant with a small disco area and had set up a buffet of sandwiches and junk food (which has only recently become popular in Ireland, to the vocal despair of nutritionists). The music was ear splitting, and because they were closed into the one room, the perspiration count was at least one hundred degrees Fahrenheit. The whole program was designed to offend adults—and it worked.

There must have been some tom-tom system audible only to teenage ears because, within an hour, the house, the yard, and the neighborhood were crawling with kids who had come to see Kate off. I knew she had been gregarious and gracious all year long, but that scene was very surprising and gratifying.

The kids left around dinnertime, and shortly after, a procession of adult visitors began. The whole evening was very Irish. No sense of stress or time on the part of the well-wishers. Of course, I had my nails chewed down almost to my elbows. It seemed as though our family was in a tension bubble in the middle of serene Ireland.

I finally collapsed at 1:00 a.m. Mary didn't come up until almost 3:30.

Friday, June 28. I was back up at five and brought Mary her wake-up coffee. It remains one of the great miracles of our time that no one in the house was strangled that morning. All the patron saints of patience, family solidarity, love, justice, and tranquility were worked to the bone between 6:00-10:00 a.m.

Patti Punch arrived with her car. There were already about ten kids parked outside the house, so I put them to work loading the car. Then Dierdre drove over and we packed her car. Called Martha and she drove up. The whole place had a festive air.

We started to caravan away amidst tearful teenage good-byes and, lo and behold, Niamh had her entire pre-K school group out standing along the white driveway gate and front wall. Mary had visited the little ones several times and they wanted to see her. It was quite poignant.

Our flight was as smooth as could be. Kate was so excited about the visit home and the prospect of returning in the fall that she infected us. There was quite a contrast between this flight and the one coming over here last September.

We set down in Boston about 1:30 EDT—six hours and at least a million miles from the lifestyle we had come to love in Limerick.

Epilogue

We returned to Ireland the following September, but, alas, because of my enormously heavy commitments teaching and writing the modules for a new American Studies Department, I was not able to maintain my rigorous daily note-keeping regimen. Perhaps there is still another book in me, however — probably broader in scope and more reflective.

Our life was turned upside-down when we finally came back to the States. Kate was taken seriously ill. We sold our home in suburban Washington, D.C., and moved to Central New York, closer to our family and roots. Kate finally recovered fully, thank God.

I taught at the State University of New York at Oswego for a couple years and Mary returned to an active role in the world of Early Childhood education.

In 1997, the White House asked me to take over the regional administration of the U.S. Department of Education. I did so with equal amounts of enthusiasm and trepidation.

Since 2001, I have been very actively engaged as an education consultant.

"Lauran"

Open fields behind "Lauran"

Kate, Mary & John

**The welcoming party at Mary's Paternal Homestead
Boloughera, Lisseycasey, County Clare**

John Coakley and the Author

Mahoney and Dr. Nick Rees

John and Margaret Stapleton

The Professor and...

...the "Banger"

Entrance to the University of Limerick

Plassey House

View from John's office

Ned Ryan Og (L) with Dick "Mac" Ryan

Philip Heenan with "Tiny"

Burro-ing in the Burren

**Mary with Dierdre O'Sullivan and Niamh O'Sullivan
at the University Club on Campus**

Kate at Ashroe

Kate and John in Connor Pass on the Dingle Peninsula

Kate and John at Lough Gur

Ryan's Market in "Downtown" Anacotty

Fishermen on the Mulcair River at Anacotty

Our neighbor Tommy McNamara
Clyduff Road, Lisnagry

Railroad Gate and Gatekeeper's House, Cryduff Road Lisnagry

**Finnegan's Pub
Lisnagry, Co. Limerick**

**Tommy Berkery and Johnny Rainsford
at Finnegan's**

**John at Glenstal Abbey with
Brother Henry O'Shea**

**Mary and Kate at the
Blennerville Wind Mill**

**Mary Mahoney & Martha Laffan
at Windsurfing Competition on Lough Derg**

The Crescent Jesuit Church
O'Connell Street, Limerick

Fr. Paddy Tyrell celebrated Mass
at "Lauran" on our Wedding Anniversary

American Students celebrated Thanksgiving with us.

With our neighbors Pat and Sadie McGrath outside the Ahane Church

The Murphy Clan visited us.

(Gen) Paul & Ruth Gorman at the Cliffs of Moher

**Mary and Kate with Fr. Mick Molloy
at Tuam, County Galway**

**L-R - Betty and Martin Ryan, Bishop Harty, Mahoney, Bridget Hehir,
Fr. Minogue and Bridget's granddaughter Lorraine in front.
at Kates Confirmation in Castle Connell**

Glenstal Abbey

**Mahoney in St. Stephen's Green
Dublin**

Patti Punch loading the car for our departure

The Kids bid farewell to Mary

Double Rainbow
From the front garden at "LAURAN"